The Wild Orchids of North America, North of Mexico

Florida A&M University, Tallahassee
Florida Atlantic University, Boca Raton
Florida Gulf Coast University, Ft. Myers
Florida International University, Miami
Florida State University, Tallahassee
University of Central Florida, Orlando
University of Florida, Gainesville
University of North Florida, Jacksonville
University of South Florida, Tampa
University of West Florida, Pensacola

The Wild Orchids of North America, North of Mexico

Paul Martin Brown

Drawings by Stan Folsom

University Press of Florida

Gainesville · Tallahassee · Tampa · Boca Raton
Pensacola · Orlando · Miami · Jacksonville · Ft. Myers

08 07 06 05 04 03 c 6 5 4 3 2 1
08 07 06 05 04 03 p 6 5 4 3 2 1

ISBN 0-8130-2571-0 (cloth)
ISBN 0-8130-2572-9 (paper)

A record of cataloging-in-publication information is available
from the Library of Congress.

The University Press of Florida is the scholarly publishing agency
for the State University System of Florida, comprising Florida A&M
University, Florida Atlantic University, Florida Gulf Coast University,
Florida International University, Florida State University, University
of Central Florida, University of Florida, University of North Florida,
University of South Florida, and University of West Florida.

University Press of Florida
15 Northwest 15th Street
Gainesville, FL 32611-2079
http://www.upf.com

A Reminder

Our wild orchids are a precious resource. For that reason they should never be collected from their native habitats, either for ornaments or for home gardens. All orchids grow in association with specific fungi, and these fungi are rarely present out of the orchids' original home. Searching for and finding these choice botanical treasures is one of the greatest pleasures of both the professional and the amateur botanist. Please leave them for others to enjoy as well.

Contents

Preface   ix

Abbreviations and Symbols   xi

Checklist of the Wild Orchids   1

A Selection of Hybrids and Color, Leaf, and Growth Forms   129

Using the Checklist as a Field Guide   155

Key to the Wild Orchids   157

Appendix: Excluded Species   185

Additions, Corrections, Nomenclatural Changes, and Comments for Luer (1972), *The Native Orchids of Florida,* and Luer (1975), *The Native Orchids of the United States and Canada excluding Florida*   187

Glossary   197

Bibliography   201

Photo Credits   205

Index   207

Personal Checklist   225

Preface

Not since the 1924 publication of *An Enumeration of the Orchids of the United States and Canada* by Oakes Ames has an annotated checklist been available. Although not a checklist, Carlyle A. Luer's two-volume work (1972, 1975) on the orchids of the United States and Canada contains much-needed taxonomic work. W.J. Schrenk's (1977) checklist was reasonably comprehensive, but in addition to being generally unavailable to most orchidists, it contains some very different concepts of genera and species. The third edition of J.T. Kartesz (2000) brought a more realistic list of species, but did not deal with several newer species, genera concepts, or taxa at the forma level. This checklist has been organized to coordinate all current North American orchid taxonomic information. Literature citations are given for recently described, little known, or significantly revised taxa.

Many excellent recent works have treatments of specific genera or geographic areas that should be consulted for more information:

Coleman (1995) for *Piperia*
Garay (1982) and Catling (1989) for most of the generic changes in *Spiranthes*
Sheviak for recent work on the green-flowered *Platanthera* species
Wesley Higgins for the genus *Prosthechea*
Brown and Folsom (2002) and Hammer (2001) for Florida species

Volume 26 of the *Flora of North America,* which contains the Orchidaceae, has resulted in numerous nomenclatural changes. Those changes appear in this checklist. With rare exceptions the nomenclature in *Flora of North America* is followed, although several additional taxa are recognized as well as all published formae.

This work could not have been accomplished if it were not for the assistance of many individuals. Ken Scott and his staff at the University Press of Florida have been a constant source of encouragement. Particular thanks goes to Chuck Sheviak, Paul M. Catling, Jim Ackerman, Gustavo Romero, Ron Coleman, George Argus, Bob Dressler, Leslie Garay, Roger Hammer, Chuck McCartney, and John Kartesz for comments and suggestions. Helen Jeude, senior technical editor for the Flora of

North America Project, has been especially helpful in permitting me to cross-check synonyms and references with the treatments in preparation for volume 26 of the *Flora*. All of those friends who contributed photos are acknowledged in the photo credits section. The concept of an illustrated checklist could not have been fulfilled without Stan Folsom's complete set of drawings of all of the species, subspecies, and varieties known from North America. For those I am particularly grateful.

Abbreviations and Symbols

AOS = American Orchid Society, publishers of the *American Orchid Society Bulletin* and *Orchids* magazine: same magazine, the name changed in 1998

FNA = *Flora of North America,* volume 26, which includes the Orchidaceae

NANOJ = *North American Native Orchid Journal*

ca. = about or approximate

cf. = confer or compare to; comparable to the usage of "?" in front of a name, at the end of a name, and in between the generic name and specific epithet, indicating the doubtful affinity with that species

cm = centimeter

f. = *filius;* son of, or the younger

m = meter

mm = millimeter

nm = nothomorph; applied to subspecific hybrids involving parents at the varietal level

nom. nud. = *nomen nudum*; published without an author's name; an invalid publication

nom. illeg. = *nomen illegiticum*; an illegitimate name; published contrary to the *International Code of Botanical Nomenclature*

p.p. = *pro parte*; in part

subsp. = subspecies

var. = variety

* = indicates non-native species

× between or preceding a name denotes a hybrid or hybrid combination

1. Alabama	23. Mississippi	45. Virginia
2. Alaska	24. Missouri	46. Washington
3. Arizona	25. Montana	47. West Virginia
4. Arkansas	26. Nebraska	48. Wisconsin
5. California	27. Nevada	49. Wyoming
6. Colorado	28. New Hampshire	50. District of Columbia
7. Connecticut	29. New Jersey	
8. Delaware	30. New Mexico	51. Alberta
9. Florida	31. New York	52. British Columbia
10. Georgia	32. North Carolina	53. Manitoba
11. Idaho	33. North Dakota	54. New Brunswick
12. Illinois	34. Ohio	55. Newfoundland and Labrador
13. Indiana	35. Oklahoma	56. Northwest Territories
14. Iowa	36. Oregon	57. Nunavut Territories
15. Kansas	37. Pennsylvania	58. Nova Scotia
16. Kentucky	38. Rhode Island	59. Ontario
17. Louisiana	39. South Carolina	60. Prince Edward Island
18. Maine	40. South Dakota	61. Quebec
19. Maryland	41. Tennessee	62. Saskatchewan
20. Massachusetts	42. Texas	63. Yukon
21. Michigan	43. Utah	
22. Minnesota	44. Vermont	64. Greenland (Denmark)
		65. St. Pierre & Miquelon (France)

Checklist of the Wild Orchids

Each entry is arranged thusly:

genus species (author) author subspecies/variety (author) author
   synonyms
   misapplied names
common name
range
   forma(e)
references
comments

Synonyms and misapplied names are given for those in use throughout the twentieth century. More extensive listings of synonyms are given in Luer (1972, 1975). The International Plant Names Index at www.ipni.org gives full references for all synonyms and misapplied names. When applicable, names are designated that are used in Correll (1950), c; Luer (1972, 1975), l; Petrie (1981), p; Williams, Williams, and Arlott (1983), w; *Flora of North America* (vol. 26, 2002), f, for synonyms and misapplied names.

Common names can often be regional or, in a few cases, simply transliterations. The most frequently accepted common names are used.

Ranges given are for reference only and do not imply precise distribution or extant populations.

Synonyms are not given for formae, although many of them are the result of new combinations from taxa that were originally or previously recognized at the varietal level. The individual references usually cover information on those transfers.

References are for original publications, transfers, and/or recent distributional and taxonomic information.

Comments are directly referable to this species only. Illustrations are not intended to be to scale.

Amerorchis rotundifolia (Banks *ex* Pursh) Hultén

Orchis rotundifolia Banks *ex* Pursh c

small round-leaved orchis

Alaska east to Newfoundland and Greenland, south to Montana and Wyoming, Minnesota east to Maine

    forma *angustifolia* Rousseau— narrow-leaved form

    forma *beckettiae* (Boivin) Hultén— white-flowered form

    forma *immaculata* Mazurski & L.P. Johnson—white-lipped form

    forma *lineata* (Mousley) Hultén— lined-lip form

Brown, P.M. 1995. *NANOJ* 1(2): 132.
Johnson, L.P. 1995. *Lindleyana* 10(1): 1.

locally abundant in the north and west, very rare in the east

Aplectrum hyemale (Mühlenberg *ex* Willdenow) Nuttall

putty-root, Adam-and-Eve

Minnesota and Ontario east to Vermont and Massachusetts, south to Arkansas and Georgia

    forma *pallidum* House—yellow-flowered form

local in the northern portion of the range, becoming more frequent southward; leaf withering at flowering time

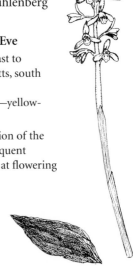

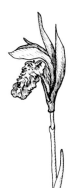

Arethusa bulbosa Linnaeus

dragon's-mouth

Saskatchewan east to Newfoundland, south to Indiana and South Carolina
    forma *albiflora* Rand & Redfield— white-flowered form
    forma *subcaerulea* Rand & Redfield—lilac-blue-flowered form

locally abundant in the northern portion of the range; becoming much rarer southward

Basiphyllaea corallicola (Small) Ames

> *Basiphyllaea angustifolia* Schlechter
> *Carteria corallicola* Small

Carter's orchid

southeastern Florida; the Bahamas, West Indies

Hammer, R.L. 1992. *Fairchild Tropical Garden Bulletin.* 47(2): 34–39.

McCartney, C.L., Jr. 1991. *Florida Orchidist.* 34(4): 136–57.

———. 1992. *Florida Orchidist.* 35(1): 195–211.

elusive and not appearing every year

Beloglottis costaricensis
(Reichenbach *f.*) Schlechter

Spiranthes costaricensis
Reichenbach *f.* L, W

Costa Rican ladies'-tresses

southeastern Florida; West Indies,
Central America, (northern South
America?)

well established within Everglades
National Park, Florida

Bletia florida (Salisbury)
R. Brown*

slender pine-pink

southeastern Florida; West Indies
Hammer, R. 2001. *NANOJ* 7(1): 70.

adventive near Homestead, Florida

Bletia patula Graham*

Haitian pine-pink

southeastern Florida; West Indies

single collection from Miami-Dade County,
Florida, in 1947

Bletia purpurea (Lamark) de Candolle

pine-pink

southern Florida; West Indies, Mexico, Central America,
northern South America

    forma *alba* (Ariza-Julia & J. Jiménez Alm.) P.M. Brown—
white-flowered form

Brown, P.M. 2000. *NANOJ* 6(4): 337.

widespread and frequent in the southern third of Florida;
possibly adventive northward

Bletilla striata (Thunberg) Reichenbach *f.**

urn orchid

northwestern Florida; Asia

single record as an escape in Escambia County, Florida

Brassia caudata (Linnaeus) Lindley

spider orchid

southeastern Florida; West Indies, Mexico, Central America, northern South America

presumed extirpated from Everglades National Park, Florida; last seen in the late 1960s

Bulbophyllum pachyrachis (A. Richard) Grisebach

rat-tail orchid

southwestern Florida; West Indies, Mexico, Central America, northern South America

presumed extirpated from Fakahatchee Strand State Preserve, Florida; last seen in 1972?

Calopogon barbatus (Walter) Ames

   Limodorum parviflorum (Lindley) Nash

bearded grass-pink

North Carolina south to Florida, west to Louisiana

the earliest of the grass-pinks to flower throughout its range

Calopogon multiflorus
Lindley

Calopogon barbatus (Walter)
Ames var. *multiflorus* (Lindley)
Correll

Limodorum multiflorum
(Lindley) C. Mohr

Limodorum pinetorum Small

many-flowered grass-pink

North Carolina south to Florida, west to eastern Louisiana
Goldman, D.H., and S. Orzell.
2000. *Lindleyana* 15(4):
237–51.

becoming very rare and local;
fire respondent

Calopogon oklahomensis D.H.
Goldman

Oklahoma grass-pink

southern Minnesota and southern Indiana south to eastern
Texas and west-central Louisiana; east to South Carolina
Brown, P.M. 1995. *NANOJ* 1(2):
133.
Goldman, D.H. 1995.
Lindleyana 10(1): 37–42.

widespread and local in scattered locales; overlooked as a
species for many years

Calopogon pallidus
Chapman

> *Limodorum pallidum*
> (Chapman) C. Mohr

pale grass-pink

Virginia south to Florida, west
to Louisiana
> forma *albiflorus* P.M.
> Brown—white-flowered form
> Brown, P.M. 1995. *NANOJ*
>   1(1): 8.

widespread and frequently
common

Calopogon tuberosus (Linnaeus) Britton, Sterns, & Poggenberg var.
tuberosus

> *Calopogon pulchellus* (Salisbury) R. Brown c
> *Calopogon pulchellus* (Salisbury) R. Brown var. *latifolius* (St. John) Fernald
> *Calopogon tuberosus* (Linnaeus) Britton, Sterns, & Poggenberg var. *latifolius*
> (St. John) Boivin
> *Limodorum tuberosum* Linnaeus

common grass-pink

Manitoba east to Newfoundland, south to Florida, west to Texas
> forma *albiflorus* Britton—white-flowered form
Catling, P.M., and Z. Lucas. 1987. *Rhodora* 89: 401–13.

widespread and often abundant throughout all of its range

Calopogon tuberosus (Linnaeus) Britton, Sterns, & Poggenberg var. *simpsonii* (Small) Magrath

Calopogon pulchellus (Salisbury) R. Brown var. *simpsonii* (Small) Ames
Limodorum simpsonii (Chapman) Small

Simpson's grass-pink

southern Florida; West Indies
forma *niveus* P.M. Brown—white-flowered form
Brown, P.M. 1995. *NANOJ* 1(2): 130.
Magrath, L.K., and J.L. Norman. 1989. *Sida* 13(3): 371–72.

a distinctive variety limited to the marls of southern Florida

Calypso bulbosa (Linnaeus) Oakes var. *americana* (R. Brown) Luer

Cytherea bulbosa (Linnaeus) House *p.p.*

eastern fairy-slipper

Alaska east to Newfoundland, south in the Rocky Mountains; south to the upper Great Lakes and northern New England
forma *albiflora* P.M. Brown—white-flowered form
forma *rosea* P.M. Brown—pink-flowered form
Brown, P.M. 1995. *NANOJ* 1(1): 17.

becoming very rare in the southeastern portion of the range, although locally abundant in the west

Calypso bulbosa (Linnaeus) Oakes var.
occidentalis (Holtzinger) B. Boivin

    Calypso bulbosa subsp. *occidentalis* (Holzinger)
Calder & Taylor

western fairy-slipper

Alaska south to central California, east to western
Montana

    forma *nivea* Brown & Coleman—white-
flowered form

Brown, P.M. 1995. *NANOJ* 1(1): 17.
Coleman, R.A. 1992. *AOS Bulletin*
   61(8): 776–81/fc.

widespread and locally abundant,
especially in the redwood regions
of California

*Campylocentrum
pachyrrhizum*
(Reichenbach *f.*) Rolfe

crooked-spur orchid

southwestern Florida; West
Indies, northern South
America

restricted to the Fakahatchee/
Big Cypress area of Florida

Cephalanthera austiniae
(A. Gray) Heller

> *Eburophyton austinae*
> (A. Gray) Heller

phantom orchid

southern British Columbia south
to California, east to Idaho
Catling, P.M., and C.J. Sheviak.
1993. *Lindleyana* 8(2): 79.

unmistakable coloration makes
identification easy

Cleistes bifaria (Fernald) Catling
& Gregg

> *Cleistes divaricata* (Linnaeus) Ames
> var. *bifaria* Fernald P, w
> *Pogonia bifaria* (Fernald) P.M.
> Brown & Wunderlin

upland spreading pogonia

West Virginia south to Florida, west
to eastern Texas
Brown, P.M., and R. Wunderlin. 1997.
NANOJ 3(4): 450–52.
Catling, P.M., and K.B. Gregg. 1992.
Lindleyana 7(2): 57–73.

smaller in stature and paler in color
than *C. divaricata*

Cleistes divaricata (Linnaeus) Ames

> *Pogonia divaricata* (Linnaeus) R. Brown *ex* Aiton *f.*

spreading pogonia

New Jersey south to Florida
> forma *leucantha* P.M. Brown—
white-flowered form
Brown, P.M. 1995. *NANOJ* 1(1): 7.
Catling, P.M., and K.B. Gregg. 1992.
> *Lindleyana* 7(2): 57–73.

one of the most striking orchids of the southeastern coastal plain

Coeloglossum viride (Linnaeus) Hartman var. *viride*

> *Coeloglossum viride* (Linnaeus) Hartman var. *islandicum* (Lindley) Schulze
> *Dactylorhiza viridis* (Linnaeus) R.M. Bateman, A. Pridgeon, & M.W. Chase
> *Habenaria viridis* (Linnaeus) R. Brown *ex* Aiton *f.* C

northern bracted green orchis

Alaska east to Newfoundland; Eurasia
Bateman, R.M., A.M. Pridgeon, and
> M.W. Chase. 1997. *Lindleyana* 12(3): 129.

widespread and scattered, although easily overlooked.

Coeloglossum viride (Linnaeus) Hartman var. *virescens* (Mühlenberg) Luer

    Coeloglossum bracteatum (Mühlenberg *ex* Willdenow) Parlin

    Coeloglossum viride (Linnaeus) Hartman subsp. *bracteatum* (Mühlenberg *ex* Willdenow) Hultén

    Habenaria bracteata (Mühlenberg *ex* Willdenow) R. Brown *ex* Aiton *f.*

    Habenaria viridis Linnaeus var. *bracteata* (Mühlenberg *ex* Willdenow) Reichenbach *ex* Gray c

    Habenaria viridis Linnaeus var. *interjecta* Fernald

long bracted green orchis

Alaska east to Newfoundland, south to Washington, New Mexico, Iowa, and North Carolina

widespread but rarely frequent; usually as individuals or small colonies

Corallorhiza bentleyi Freudenstein

Bentley's coralroot

western Virginia and southeastern West Virginia

Bentley, S. 2000. *Native Orchids of the Southern Appalachians,* pp. 71–75.

———. 2001. *NANOJ* 7(2): 140–42.

Freudenstein, J.V. 1999. *Novon* 9(4): 511–13.

one of the most recently described species in North America; unlike any other *Corallorhiza*

Corallorhiza maculata (Rafin-esque) Rafinesque var. *maculata*

  Corallorhiza multiflora Nuttall

spotted coralroot

British Columbia east to Newfound-land, south to California, Arizona, and New Mexico; Appalachian Mts. south to northern Georgia and South Carolina

  forma *flavida* (Peck) Farwell—yellow-stemmed form

  forma *rubra* P.M. Brown—red-stemmed form

Brown, P.M. 1995. *NANOJ* 1(1): 8.

widespread and often in colorful colonies; flowers later than var. *occidentalis*

Corallorhiza maculata (Rafin-esque) Rafinesque var. *mexicana* (Lindley) Freudenstein

  Corallorhiza mexicana Lindley

Mexican spotted coralroot

Arizona; Mexico, Guatemala

Coleman, R.A. 2002. *Wild Orchids of Arizona and New Mexico*, p. 39.

Freudenstein, J. 1997. *Harvard Papers in Botany* 10: 5–51.

recently determined from a population in Pima County, Arizona

Corallorhiza maculata (Rafinesque) Rafinesque var. *occidentalis* (Lindley) Ames

Corallorhiza maculata subsp. *occidentalis* (Lindley) Cockerell

western spotted coralroot

British Columbia east to Newfoundland, south to California, Arizona, New Mexico, Indiana, and Virginia

forma *aurea* P.M. Brown—golden yellow/spotted form

forma *immaculata* (Peck) Howell—yellow spotless form

forma *intermedia* Farwell—brown-stemmed form

forma *punicea* (Bartholomew) Weatherby & Adams—red-stemmed form

Brown, P.M. 1995. *NANOJ* 1(3): 195.

Freudenstein, J.V. 1986. *Contributions from the University of Michigan Herbarium* 16: 145–53.

———. 1997. *Harvard Papers in Botany* 10: 5–51.

larger and earlier flowering than var. *maculata;* some of the forms have been previously published as varieties

Corallorhiza mertensiana Bongard

Corallorhiza maculata subsp. *mertensiana* (Bongard) Calder & Taylor

Corallorhiza purpurea L.O. Williams

western coralroot

southern Alaska south to California, east to Montana and western Wyoming

forma *albolabia* P.M. Brown—white-flowered form

forma *pallida* P.M. Brown—pale colored form

Brown, P.M. 1995. *NANOJ* 1(1): 9.

———. 1995. *NANOJ* 1(3): 197.

the most frequently encountered of the coralroots in the Pacific Northwest

Corallorhiza odontorhiza
(Willdenow) Nuttall var.
odontorhiza

Corallorhiza micrantha Chapman

autumn coralroot

South Dakota east to Ontario, Quebec, and Maine, south to Arizona and Florida
forma *flavida* Wherry—yellow-stemmed form

the cleistogamous flowers combined with the small stature and lateness of flowering make this variety easily overlooked

Corallorhiza odontorhiza (Willdenow) Nuttall var. *pringlei* (Greenman) Freudenstein

Corallorhiza pringlei Greenman

Pringle's autumn coralroot

Wisconsin and Ontario east to Maine, south to Iowa, Tennessee, and Georgia; Mexico, Central America
Freudenstein, J.V. 1993. Dissertation. Cornell University.
———. 1997. *Harvard Papers in Botany* 10: 5–51.

the larger chasmogamous flowers make this variety more attractive than var. *odontorhiza*

Corallorhiza striata Lindley var. *striata*

striped coralroot

British Columbia east to Newfoundland, south to California,
Texas, and New York
    forma *eburnea* P.M. Brown—
yellow/white form
Brown, P.M. 1995. *NANOJ* 1(1): 9.

the largest flowered and most striking of all of the coralroots

Corallorhiza striata Lindley var. *vreelandii* (Rydberg) L.O. Williams

    Corallorhiza bigelovii S. Watson
    Corallorhiza striata Lindley forma
fulva Fernald

Vreeland's striped coralroot

California east to South Dakota, south
to New Mexico; Quebec; Mexico
    forma *flavida* (Todson & Todson)
P.M. Brown—yellow/white form
Brown, P.M. 1995. *NANOJ* 1(1): 14.

the smaller flowers and paler coloring
are distinctive field marks

Corallorhiza trifida Chatelain

Corallorhiza corallorhiza
(Linnaeus) MacMillan
Corallorhiza trifida Chatelain var.
verna (Nuttall) Fernald

early coralroot

Alaska east to Newfoundland and
Greenland, south to California, south
in Rocky Mts., east to New England
and West Virginia; Eurasia

the earliest to flower of the northern
species of coralroot; color varies
from chartreuse green to yellow and
to bronze in the northernmost areas

Corallorhiza wisteriana Conrad

Wister's coralroot

Washington east to New Jersey, south to
Arizona and Florida; Mexico
    forma *albolabia* P.M. Brown—white-
flowered form
    forma *rubra* P.M. Brown—red-
stemmed form
Brown, P.M. 1995. *NANOJ* 1(1): 9–10.
————. 2000. *NANOJ* 6(1): 62.

the most frequently encountered of the
southeastern species of coralroot; flowering starts in January in Florida

Cranichis muscosa Swartz

moss-loving cranichis

southern Florida; West Indies,
Mexico, Central America,
northern South America

no collections or confirmed
sightings for nearly 100 years

Cyclopogon cranichoides
(Grisebach) Schlechter

 Beadlea cranichoides (Grisebach)
Small
 Spiranthes cranichoides (Grisebach)
Cogniaux c, l, w

speckled ladies'-tresses

Florida; the Bahamas, West Indies,
Central America, South America
 forma *albolabius* (Brown &
McCartney) P.M. Brown—white-
lipped form
Brown, P.M. 1995. *NANOJ* 1(1): 8.
———. 1998. *NANOJ* 4(1): 52.

widespread and local in Florida;
historically more abundant

Cyclopogon elatus (Swartz) Schlechter

> *Beadlea elata* (Swartz) Small
> *Spiranthes elata* (Swartz) L.C. Richard C, L, W

tall neottia

Florida; West Indies, Mexico, Central America, northern South America

no recent reports and very few historical records in Florida

Cypripedium acaule Aiton

> *Fissipes acaulis* (Aiton) Small

pink lady's-slipper, moccasin flower

Northwest Territories east to Newfoundland, south to Minnesota and Georgia

> forma *albiflorum* Rand & Redfield—white-flowered form
> forma *biflorum* P.M. Brown—two-flowered form
> Brown, P.M. 1995. *NANOJ* 1(3): 197.

the most familiar lady's-slipper of the eastern acidic forests

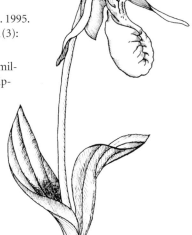

Cypripedium arietinum R. Brown

Criosanthes arietina (Aiton *f.*) House

ram's-head lady's-slipper

Saskatchewan east to Nova Scotia, south to Massachusetts

forma *albiflorum* House—white-flowered form

forma *biflorum* P.M. Brown—two-flowered form

Brown, P.M. 1995.

NANOJ 1(3): 198.

becoming rare and local except around the upper Great Lakes region

Cypripedium californicum Gray

California lady's-slipper

southern Oregon south to central California

widespread within a restricted range; perhaps our only orchid that is a serpentophile

Cypripedium candidum Mühlenberg *ex* Willdenow

small white lady's-slipper

Saskatchewan south to Minnesota, east to western New York, south to Missouri, Alabama, and New Jersey

rapidly disappearing from its prairie and fen habitat

Cypripedium fasciculatum Kellogg *ex* S. Watson

    Cypripedium knightiae A. Nelson

clustered lady's-slipper

Washington south to California, east to Montana and south to Colorado

Brownell, V.R., and P.M. Catling. 1987. *Lindleyana* 2(1): 53–57.

Elliman, T., and A. Dalton. 1995. *NANOJ* 1(1): 59–73.

widespread and not infrequent within the main body of the range

Cypripedium guttatum
Swartz

spotted lady's-slipper

Alaska east to Northwest Territories; Siberia

found primarily on the Alaskan mainland

Cypripedium kentuckiense C.F. Reed

Cypripedium daultonii nom. nud. P

ivory-lipped lady's-slipper

northeastern Virginia; Oklahoma east to Kentucky, south to eastern Texas and Georgia
　　forma *pricei*—white-flowered form

Atwood, J. T., Jr. 1984. *AOS Bulletin* 53(8): 835–41.

Brown, P.M. 1995. *NANOJ* 1(3): 255–66.

———. 1998. *NANOJ* 4(1): 45.

Reed, C. 1981. *Phytologia* 48(5):
　　426–28.

Weldy, T.W., H.T. Mlodozeniec,
　　L.E. Wallace, and M.A. Case.
　　1996. *Sida* 17(2): 423–35.

the largest of our yellow-
flowered species

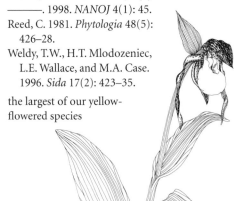

Cypripedium montanum Douglas *ex* Lindley

mountain lady's-slipper

southeastern Alaska
south to California, east
to Alberta and Wyoming
 forma *praetertinctum*
Sheviak—green-petalled
form
 forma *welchii* P.M.
Brown—crimson edge-
lipped form
Brown, P.M. 1995. *NANOJ*
 1(3): 198.
Sheviak, C.J. 1990.
 Rhodora 92: 47–49.

widespread and locally
abundant throughout its
range

Cypripedium parviflorum Salisbury var. *parviflorum*

 Cypripedium calceolus Linnaeus var. *parviflorum* (Salisbury) Fernald *p.p.* w

southern small yellow lady's-slipper

Kansas east to Massachusetts, south to Louisiana
and Georgia
 forma *albolabium* Magrath &
Norman—white-lipped form
Magrath, L.K., and J.L.
 Norman. 1989.
 Sida 13(3): 371–
 72.
Sheviak, C.J. 1994. *AOS*
 Bulletin 63(6): 664–69.
 ———. 1995. *AOS Bulle-*
 tin 64(6): 606–12.
 ———. 1996. *NANOJ*
 2(4): 319–43.

widespread and local, of-
ten misidentified

Cypripedium parviflorum Salisbury var. *makasin* (Farwell) Sheviak

Cypripedium calceolus Linnaeus var. *parviflorum* Salisbury *p.p.* L, W

C. pubescens Willdenow var. *makasin* Farwell

northern small yellow lady's-slipper

Alaska south to northern California, east to Newfoundland, south to Iowa and New Jersey

Sheviak, C.J. 1993. *AOS Bulletin* 62(4): 403.

———. 1994. *AOS Bulletin* 63(6): 664–69.

———. 1995. *AOS Bulletin* 64(6): 606–12.

———. 1996. *NANOJ* 2(4): 319–43.

widespread and locally abundant in the northern portion of its range

Cypripedium parviflorum Salisbury var. *pubescens* (Willdenow) Knight

Cypripedium calceolus Linnaeus var. *planipetalum* (Fernald) Victorin & Rousseau L, W

Cypripedium calceolus Linnaeus var. *pubescens* (Willdenow) Correll C, L, W

Cypripedium flavescens de Candolle

Cypripedium parviflorum Salisbury var. *planipetalum* Fernald

Cypripedium pubescens Willdenow

Cypripedium veganum Cockerell & Barber

Cypripedium calceolus Linnaeus misapplied C

large yellow lady's-slipper

Alaska east to Newfoundland, south to Arizona and Georgia

Sheviak, C.J. 1994. *AOS Bulletin* 63(6): 664–69.

———. 1995. *AOS Bulletin* 64(6): 606–12.

———. 1996. *NANOJ* 2(4): 319–43.

the most frequently encountered of all the yellow-flowered species; highly variable

Cypripedium passerinum Richardson

   Cypripedium passerinum Richardson var. *minganense* Victorin

sparrow's egg lady's-slipper, Franklin's lady's-slipper

Alaska east to Quebec, south to northern Montana

this small-flowered gem is frequent only in Alaska; very local and rare eastward

Cypripedium reginae Walter

   Cypripedium spectabile Salisbury

showy lady's-slipper

Saskatchewan east to Newfoundland, south to Arkansas and southern North Carolina

   forma *albolabium* Fernald & Schubert—white-flowered form

the largest of all of the lady's-slippers, it can form colonies of 10,000+ in the northern portions of its range; rare and local southward

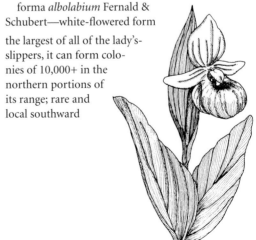

Cypripedium yatabeanum Makino

Cypripedium guttatum Swartz subsp. *yatabeanum* (Makino) Hultén

Cypripedium guttatum Swartz var. *yatabeanum* (Makino) Pfitzer L, W

yellow spotted lady's-slipper

Alaska; Siberia, northern Japan

Brown, P.M. 1995. *NANOJ* 1(3): 199.

found primarily on Kodiak Island and sparingly elsewhere

Hybrids:

Cypripedium ×alaskanum P.M. Brown

Alaskan hybrid spotted lady's-slipper

(*C. guttatum* × *C. yatabeanum*)

Brown, P.M. 1995. *NANOJ* 1(3): 199.

Cypripedium ×andrewsii Fuller nm *andrewsii*

Andrews' hybrid lady's-slipper

(*C. candidum* × *C. parviflorum* var. *makasin*)

Cypripedium ×andrewsii Fuller nm *favillianum* (Curtis) Boivin

Cypripedium ×favillianum Curtis C, L

Faville's hybrid lady's-slipper

(*C. candidum* × *C. parviflorum* var. *pubescens*)

Cypripedium ×andrewsii nm *landonii* (Garay) Boivin

Cypripedium ×landonii Garay L

Landon's hybrid lady's-slipper

(*C. candidum* × *C. ×andrewsii* nm *favillianum*)

Cypripedium ×columbianum Sheviak

Columbia hybrid lady's-slipper

(*C. parviflorum* × *C. montanum*)

Sheviak, C.J. 1992. *AOS Bulletin* 61(6): 546–59.

Cyrtopodium polyphyllum (Vell) Pabst *ex* F. Barrios*

> *Cyrtopodium paranaense* Schlechter
> *Cyrtopodium andersonii* (Lambert *ex* Andrews) R. Brown misapplied L, w
> *Cyrtopodium glutiniferum* Raddi misapplied

yellow cowhorn orchid

Florida; South America

naturalized in Miami-Dade and Highlands Counties, Florida

Cyrtopodium punctatum (Linnaeus) Lindley

cowhorn orchid, cigar orchid

Florida; Mexico, Central America, West Indies, South America

widespread in southern Florida; formerly more abundant

Dactylorhiza aristata (Fischer *ex* Lindley) Soo var. *aristata*

Orchis aristata Fischer *ex* Lindley c

Fischer's orchid

Alaska; northeastern Asia
    forma *alba* P.M. Brown—white-flowered form
Brown, P.M. 1995. *NANOJ* 1(1): 9.

found primarily along southern coastal Alaska and sparingly on Kodiak Island

Dactylorhiza aristata (Fischer *ex* Lindley) Soo var. *kodiakensis* Luer & Luer *f.*

Kodiak orchid

Alaska
    forma *rosea* P.M. Brown—pink-flowered form
    forma *perbracteata* (Lepage) P.M. Brown—leafy, flowerless form
        Brown, P.M. 1995. *NANOJ* 1(3): 199, 241.
        ———. 1996. *NANOJ* 2(1): 101.
        Ospina H., M. 1997. *NANOJ* 3(3): 293–97.

        found primarily on Kodiak and other islands in southwestern Alaska

Dactylorhiza majalis (Reichenbach) P.F. Hunt & Summerhayes var. *junialis* (Vermeulen) Senghas

 Dactylorhiza majalis (Reichenbach) P.F. Hunt & Summerhayes

 Dactylorhiza majalis (Reichenbach) Summerhayes subsp. *praetermissa* (Druce) D.M. Moore & Soo var. *junialis* (Vermeulen) Senghas

 Dactylorhiza praetermissa (Druce) Soo var. *junialis* (Vermeulen) Senghas

 Dactylorhiza comosa subsp. *majalis* (Reichenbach) P.D. Sell misapplied

 Dactylorhiza cf. *fuchsii* (Druce) Soo misapplied

 Dactylorhiza maculata (Linnaeus) Soo misapplied L, P, W

leopard marsh orchid

Ontario, Newfoundland; Europe
Catling, P.M., and C.J. Sheviak. 1993.
 Lindleyana 8(2): 80–81.
Clase, H.J., and S.J. Meades. 1996. *NANOJ* 2(3): 208–17.

known from a few sites near Timmins, Ontario; presumed introduced and persisting since 1960; discovered in 1996 near St. John's, Newfoundland; escape or introduction?

Dactylorhiza majalis (Reichenbach) Summerhayes subsp. *praetermissa* (Druce) D.M. Moore & Soo

 Dactylorhiza praetermissa (Druce) Soo var. *praetermissa*

southern marsh orchid

Newfoundland; Europe
 forma *albiflora* (Druce) P.M. Brown—white-flowered form
Brown, P.M. 2001. *NANOJ* 7(2): 186.
Catling, P.M., and C.J. Sheviak. 1993.
 Lindleyana 8(2): 80–81.
Meades, S. 1994. *Saraccenia* 5(1): 13–15.
———. 1995. *NANOJ* 1(3): 245.

known from in and around Tilt Cove, Newfoundland; reported for more than 75 years; native, introduction, or escape?

Deiregyne confusa Garay

Schiedeella confusa (Garay) Espejo & López-Ferrari
Spiranthes confusa (Garay) Kartesz & Gandhi
Deiregyne durangensis (Ames & Schweinfurth) Garay
misapplied
Spiranthes durangensis Ames & Schweinfurth
misapplied C, L, P, W

Hildago ladies'-tresses

southern Texas; Mexico

known only from the original collection
in the Chisos Mts. of Texas in 1931;
presumed extirpated

Dendrophylax lindenii (Lindley) Bentham *ex* Rolfe

Polyradicion lindenii (Lindley) Garay
Polyrrhiza lindenii (Lindley) Cogniaux C, L, W

ghost orchid, frog orchid, palm polly

southern Florida;
Cuba

the most spectacular
of the leafless species
of epiphytic orchids
in North America

Dichromanthus cinnabarinus (Llave & Lexarza) Garay

   Spiranthes cinnabarina (Llave & Lexarza) Hemsley C, L, P, W

   Stenorrhynchos cinnabarina (Llave & Lexarza) Lindley

cinnabar ladies'-tresses

southern Texas; Mexico

restricted to the Big Bend area

Eltroplectris calcarata (Swartz) Garay & Sweet

   Centrogenium setaceum (Lindley) Schlechter C, L, W

      Pelexia setacea Lindley

      Spiranthes calcarata (Swartz) Jimenez

      Stenorrhynchus calcaratus (Swartz) L.C. Richard

spurred neottia

Florida; the Bahamas, West Indies, northern South America

flights of more than a dozen delicate egret-like blossoms adorn the tall stems of this showy terrestrial

Encyclia rufa (Lindley) Britton & Millspaugh

Encyclia bahamensis (Grisebach) Britton & Millspaugh

Epidendrum bahamense Grisebach

Epidendrum rufum Lindley

rufous butterfly orchid

east-central Florida; the Bahamas

two historic collections in 1926 near Melbourne, Florida; presumed extirpated

Encyclia tampensis (Lindley) Small

Epidendrum tampense Lindley C

Florida butterfly orchid

Florida; the Bahamas
   forma *albolabia* (Hawkes) Christensen— white-lipped form

widespread throughout central and southern Florida; one of the showiest and most popular species

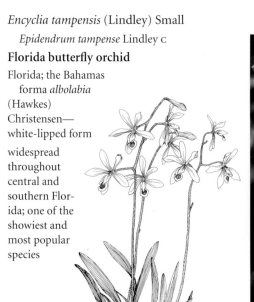

Epidendrum acunae Dressler

Epidendrum blancheanum Urban misapplied

Acuña's star orchid

southwestern Florida; Cuba, Central America

known from a single locality in Florida's
Fakahatchee Swamp; not seen in recent years

Epidendrum amphistomum A. Richard

Epidendrum anceps Jacquin misapplied c, l, w

dingy-flowered star orchid

southern Florida; West Indies,
Central America, northern
South America
　forma *rubrifolium* P.M.
Brown—red-leaved form
Brown, P.M. 2000. *NANOJ*
　6(1): 61.
Hágsater, E. 2000.
　NANOJ 6(4): 300–10.

widespread and often
frequent in
southernmost
counties of Florida

Epidendrum floridense Hágsater

Epidendrum difforme Jacquin misapplied c, l, w
Neolehmannia difformis (Jacquin) Pabst misapplied

Florida star orchid

southern Florida; Cuba
Hágsater, E. 2000. *NANOJ* 6(4): 300–310.
Hágsater, E., and G. Salazar.
1993. *Icones
Orchidacearum.*
Romero, G.A. 1994. *AOS
Bulletin* 63(10):
1168–70.

a near-endemic
that was
thought to be
extirpated but
is making an
excellent return

Epidendrum magnoliae
Mühlenberg var. *magnoliae*

Epidendrum conopseum R.
Brown var. *conopseum* c, l, w

green-fly orchis

southeastern North Carolina
south to Florida, west to
Louisiana
Hágsater, E. 2000. *NANOJ* 6(4):
300–310.

northernmost species of epiphytic orchid in North
America

Epidendrum magnoliae Mühlenberg var.
mexicanum (L.O. Williams) P.M. Brown

    Epidendrum conopseum R. Brown var. *mexicanum*
L.O. Williams

bronze green-fly orchis

central Florida; Mexico
Brown, P.M. 1998. *NANOJ* 5(1): 3.
————. 2000. *NANOJ* 6(4): 337–38.

more colorful and with a different
fragrance than the nominate
variety

Epidendrum nocturnum Jacquin

night-fragrant epidendrum

southern Florida; West Indies, Central America,
northern and central South America

the largest flowered of the genus in North America

Epidendrum cf. *radicans* Pavén *ex* Lindley*

climbing epidendrum

southern Florida; West Indies, Central and South America

a persistent escape at old homesites in Lee and Miami-Dade Counties, Florida

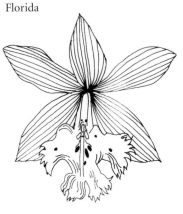

Epidendrum rigidum Jacquin

rigid epidendrum

southern Florida; West Indies, South America

a frequent species of the southern swamps, but the flowers are inconspicuous

Epidendrum strobiliferum Swartz

cone-bearing epidendrum

southern Florida; West Indies, Central America, northern and central South America

very rare and local, if not often overlooked, in southwestern Florida

Epipactis atrorubens (Hoffman *ex* Bernhardi) Besser*

Epipactis rubiginosa (Crantz) W.D.J. Koch

red helleborine

northern Vermont; Europe

known from a single site in northern Vermont growing in a serpentine area

Epipactis gigantea Douglas *ex* Hooker

Amesia gigantea (Douglas) A. Nelson & Macbride
Helleborine gigantea (Douglas) Druce

stream orchid

southern British Columbia east to South Dakota, south to California, Arizona, New Mexico, and Texas; Mexico

forma *citrina* P.M. Brown—yellow-flowered form

forma *rubrifolia* P.M. Brown—red-leaved form

Brown, P.M. 1995. *NANOJ* 1(4): 287.

———. 2001. *NANOJ* 7(4): 257.

Coleman, R.A. 1995. *Wild Orchids of California*, p. 75, pl. 13.

widespread and often abundant in the western states

Epipactis helleborine (Linnaeus) Cranz*

Epipactis latifolia (Linnaeus) Allioni

broad-leaved helleborine

eastern North America, southeastern California, scattered in western North America; Europe

forma *alba* (Webster) Boivin—white-flowered form

forma *luteola* P.M. Brown—yellow-flowered form

forma *monotropoides* (Mousley) Scoggin—albino form

forma *variegata* (Webster) Boivin—variegated form

forma *viridens* A. Gray—green-flowered form

Brown, P.M. 1996. *NANOJ* 2(4): 316.

known for more than 100 years in eastern North America and now spreading throughout the midwestern and western states

Eulophia alta (Linnaeus) Fawcett & Rendle

Platypus altus (Linnaeus) Small

wild coco

Georgia south to Florida; Mexico, West Indies, Central America, South America, Africa

forma *pallida* P.M. Brown— pale-colored form

forma *pelchatii* P.M. Brown— white and green-flowered form Brown, P.M. 1995 *NANOJ* 1(2): 131.

————. 1998 *NANOJ* 4(1): 46.

widespread throughout all of Florida, often in wet roadside ditches

Galeandra bicarinata G.A. Romero & P.M. Brown.

Galeandra beyrichii Reichenbach *f.* misapplied c, l, w

two keeled galeandra

southeastern Florida; Cuba Romero, G.A., and P.M. Brown. 2000. *NANOJ* 6(2): 77–87.

recently described; known only from a few sites in and near Everglades National Park, Florida

Galearis spectabilis (Linnaeus) Rafinesque

Galeorchis spectabilis (Linnaeus) Rydberg
Orchis spectabilis Linnaeus c

showy orchis

Minnesota east to New Brunswick, south to
eastern Oklahoma and Georgia
    forma *gordinierii* (House) Whiting &
Catling—white-flowered form
    forma *willeyi* (Seymour) P.M. Brown—
pink-flowered form
Brown, P.M. 1988. *Wild
    Flower Notes* 3(1): 20.

widespread through the
central and southern
states within its range,
usually in circum-
neutral soils

Goodyera oblongifolia Rafinesque

Goodyera decipiens (Hooker) F.T.
Hubbard

giant rattlesnake orchis

southeastern Alaska east to Newfoundland,
south to Maine, California, and New
Mexico; Mexico
    forma *reticulata* (Boivin) P.M. Brown—
reticulated-leaved form
Brown, P.M. 1995. *NANOJ* 1(1): 14.

rare and local in the east; widespread and
often abundant in the west

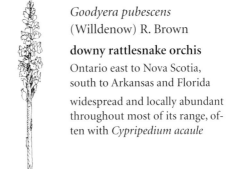

Goodyera pubescens
(Willdenow) R. Brown

downy rattlesnake orchis

Ontario east to Nova Scotia,
south to Arkansas and Florida

widespread and locally abundant
throughout most of its range, often with *Cypripedium acaule*

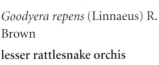

Goodyera repens (Linnaeus) R.
Brown

lesser rattlesnake orchis

Alaska east to Newfoundland, south in
the Rocky and Appalachian Mts.; northern Eurasia

    forma *ophioides* (Fernald) P.M.
Brown—white-veined leaf form
Brown, P.M. 1995. *NANOJ* 1(1): 14.

the forma *ophioides* is most frequently
seen except in the western and far northern portion of the range

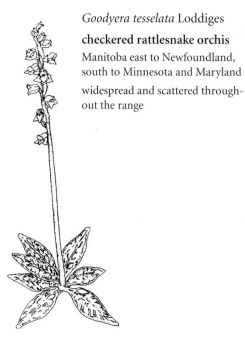

Goodyera tesselata Loddiges

checkered rattlesnake orchis

Manitoba east to Newfoundland, south to Minnesota and Maryland

widespread and scattered throughout the range

Govenia floridana P.M. Brown

Govenia utriculata (Swartz) Lindley misapplied L, w

Florida govenia

southeastern Florida

Brown, P.M. 2000. *NANOJ* 6(3): 230–40.

Greenwood, E.W. 1991. *AOS Bulletin* 60(9): 867–69.

———. 1996. *NANOJ* 2(1): 344–49.

endemic to southernmost Florida; possibly extirpated

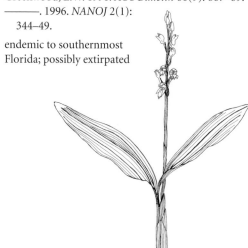

Gymnadenia conopsea
(Linnaeus) R. Brown*

  Habenaria conopsea (Linnaeus)
Bentham c

fragrant orchid

northwestern Connecticut

waif; known from a single collection
in 1887

Habenaria distans Grisebach

false water-spider orchid

southern Florida; West Indies,
Mexico, Central America, northern
South America

known from two remaining sites in
southwestern Florida; three other
sites probably extirpated

Habenaria macroceratitis Willdenow

Habenaria habenaria (Linnaeus) Small
Habenaria quinqueseta Willdenow var. *macroceratitis* (Willdenow) Luer L, W

long-horned habenaria

Florida; Mexico, Central America
Brown, P.M. 2000. *NANOJ* 6(2): 142–53.

largest and most spectacular of the genus; restricted to central Florida

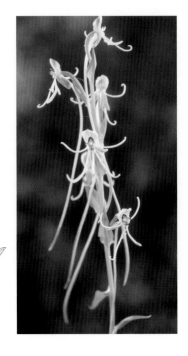

Habenaria odontopetala Reichenbach *f.*

Habenaria garberi Small
Habenaria strictissima Reichenbach *f.* var. *odontopetala* (Reichenbach *f.*) L.O. Williams C
Habenella odontopetala (Reichenbach *f.*) Small
Habenaria floribunda Lindley misapplied

toothed habenaria

Florida; Mexico, West Indies, Central America
forma *heatonii* P.M. Brown—albino form
Brown, P.M. 2001. *NANOJ* 7(1): 93–94.

one of the most common terrestrial orchids in central and southern Florida

Habenaria quinqueseta
(Michaux) Eaton

Michaux's orchid

South Carolina south to Florida,
west to Texas; West Indies, Mexico,
Central America, South America

widespread throughout Florida; rare
and local elsewhere

Habenaria repens Nuttall

> *Habenaria nuttallii* Small
> *Platanthera repens*
> (Nuttall) Wood

water spider orchid

North Carolina south to
Florida, west to southeastern
Oklahoma and Texas;
Mexico, West Indies, Central
America, South America

one of the few aquatic orchids we have in North
America

Harrisella porrecta (Reichenbach f.)
Fawcett & Rendle

   Campylocentrum porrectum
Reichenbach f.
   Harrisella filiformis (Swartz)
Cogniaux misapplied

leafless harrisella

Florida; Mexico, Central America,
West Indies

Ackerman, J.D.
   1995. *Orchids
   of Puerto Rico
   and the Virgin Is-
   lands,* p. 87.

the smallest and most
inconspicuous of the
leafless epiphytic or-
chids in Florida

Hexalectris grandiflora (A. Richard
& Galeotti) L.O. Williams

   Hexalectris mexicana
Greenman

**Greenman's crested
coralroot**

Texas; Mexico

the largest flowered and
showiest of the genus

Hexalectris nitida L.O.
Williams

**shining crested
coralroot**

Texas; Mexico

this and *H. revoluta* are
very similar and easily
confused

Hexalectris revoluta Correll

recurved crested coralroot

Arizona, Texas; Mexico
Coleman, R.A. 1999. *NANOJ*
    5(1): 312–15.

recent discoveries in Arizona
have increased the range of this
rare species

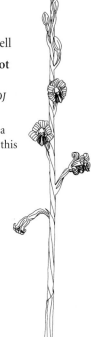

Hexalectris spicata (Walter) Barnhardt var. *spicata*

crested coralroot

Arizona east to Maryland, south to Florida and west to Texas; Mexico

 forma *albolabia* P.M. Brown—white-flowered form Brown, P.M. 1995. *NANOJ* 1(1): 10.

widespread and sporadic from year to year

Hexalectris spicata (Walter) Barnhardt var. *arizonica* (S. Watson) Catling & Engel

 Corallorhiza arizonica S. Watson

Arizona crested coralroot

Arizona east to Texas; Mexico Catling, P.M., and V.S. Engel. 1993. *Lindleyana* 8(3): 119–26.

locally scattered in the Southwest; flowers usually cleistogamous

Hexalectris warnockii
Ames & Correll

Texas purple-spike

Arizona, Texas

delicate, but the most
elegant of the genus

Ionopsis utricularioides (Swartz) Lindley

delicate ionopsis

southern Florida; West Indies, Central
America, northern South America

the showiest of the twig epiphytes

Isotria medeoloides (Pursh) Rafinesque

Isotria affinis (Austin *ex* A. Gray) Rydberg
Pogonia affinis Austin *ex* A. Gray

small whorled pogonia

Michigan east to Maine, south to
Missouri and South Carolina

federally listed as threatened;
inconspicuous in flower; rare
and local but with substantial
populations in Maine and
New Hampshire

Isotria verticillata (Mühlenberg *ex* Willdenow) Rafinesque

Pogonia verticillata (Mühlenberg *ex*
Willdenow) Nuttall

large whorled pogonia

Ontario and Michigan east to
Maine, south to Texas and
northern Florida

locally abundant throughout
its range; often with
Cypripedium acaule
and *Goodyera pubescens*

Laelia rubescens Lindley*

pale laelia

southeastern Florida; South America

waif; first seen in 1999 in Miami-Dade County, Florida

Lepanthopsis melanantha (Reichenbach *f.*) Ames

   Lepanthes harrisii Fawcett & Rendle

crimson lepanthopsis

southwestern Florida; West Indies

the rarest of the "tiny" orchids restricted to Florida's Fakahatchee/ Big Cypress area

Liparis elata Lindley

  Liparis eggersii Reichenbach *f.*
  Liparis nervosa (Thunberg) Lindley misapplied F

tall twayblade

Florida; West Indies, Mexico

a showy hemi-epiphyte with
populations in southwestern
and west-central Florida

Liparis liliifolia (Linnaeus) Richard *ex* Lindley

lily-leaved twayblade

Minnesota and Ontario east
to New Hampshire, south to
Oklahoma and Georgia
  forma *viridiflora* Wadmond—
green-flowered form

in rich woods; rare in
the northern portion of
the range, more frequent
southward

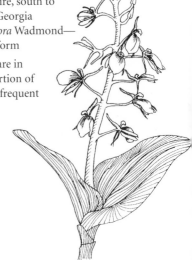

Liparis loeselii (Linnaeus) Richard

Loesel's twayblade, fen orchis

British Columbia east to Nova Scotia, south to Arkansas and Mississippi and in the southern Appalachian Mts.; Europe

often colonizing damp, disturbed areas

Hybrid:

Liparis ×jonesii S. Bentley

Jones' hybrid twayblade

(*L. liliifolia* × *L. loeselii*)
Bentley, S. 2000. *Native Orchids of the Southern Appalachians*, pp. 138–39.

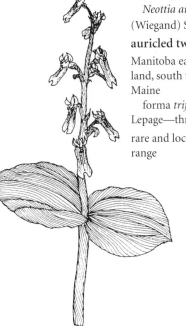

Listera auriculata Wiegand

  Neottia auriculata (Wiegand) Szlachetko

auricled twayblade

Manitoba east to Newfoundland, south to Michigan and Maine

  forma *trifolia* (Lepage) Lepage—three-leaved form

rare and local throughout its range

Listera australis Lindley

   Neottia australis (Lindley) Szlachetko

southern twayblade

Ontario east to Nova Scotia, south to Florida and west to Texas

   forma *scottii* P.M. Brown— many-leaved form

   forma *trifolia* P.M. Brown— three-leaved form

   forma *viridis* P.M. Brown— green-flowered form

Brown, P.M. 1995. *NANOJ* 1(1): 11.

————. 2000. *NANOJ* 6(1): 63–64.

rare in the northern portion of its range, becoming locally abundant southward

Listera borealis Morong

   Neottia borealis (Morong) Szlachetko

northern twayblade

Alaska east to Newfoundland, south to Utah and Colorado

   forma *trifolia* Lepage—three-leaved form

very rare and local in the east, becoming occasional westward

Listera caurina Piper

Neottia caurina (Piper) Szlachetko

northwestern twayblade

southern Alaska east to Alberta, south to California and Wyoming

frequent in the Pacific Northwest with a disjunct site on Kodiak Island, Alaska

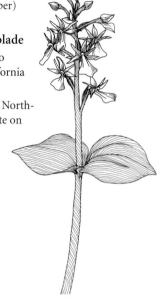

Listera convallarioides (Swartz) Nuttall

broad-lipped twayblade

southwestern Alaska; British Columbia east to Newfoundland, south to California and Arizona, east to northern Michigan and Maine

forma *trifolia* P.M. Brown—three-leaved form
Brown, P.M. 1995. *NANOJ* 1(1): 11.

locally abundant in mossy streamsides and woodland openings throughout its range

Listera cordata (Linnaeus) R. Brown var. *cordata*

heart-leaved twayblade

Alaska east to Newfoundland and Greenland, south to California, the Rocky Mts. in New Mexico, North Carolina in Appalachian Mts.; Eurasia

  forma *disjuncta* Lepage—alternate-leaved form

  forma *trifolia* P.M. Brown—three-leaved form

  forma *variegata* P.M. Brown—variegated-leaved form

  forma *viridens* P.M. Brown—green-flowered form

Brown, P.M. 1995. *NANOJ* 1(1): 11; 1(4): 288.

the most frequently seen *Listera* in eastern North America

Listera cordata (Linnaeus) R. Brown var. *nephrophylla* (Rydberg) Hultén

  Listera cordata (Linnaeus) R. Brown subsp. *nephrophylla* (Rydberg) A. & D. Löve

  Listera nephrophylla Rydberg

  Neottia nephrophylla (Rydberg) Szlachetko

western heart-leaved twayblade

Rocky Mts. west to California, north to Alaska

  forma *rubescens* P.M. Brown—reddish-flowered form

Brown, P.M. 1995. *NANOJ* 1(3): 240; 1(4): 288.

a larger counterpart to the nominate variety, often growing in much drier sites

Listera ovata (Linnaeus) R.
Brown *ex* W. Aiton & W.T.
Aiton*

common twayblade
southeastern Ontario; Europe
naturalized in southern Ontario

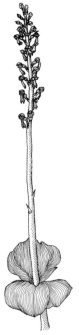

Listera smallii Wiegand
  Listera reniformis Small
  Neottia smallii (Wiegand) Szlachetko
Small's twayblade
northern New Jersey; central Pennsylvania
south to Georgia
  forma *variegata* P.M. Brown—variegated-
leaved form
Brown, P.M. 1995. *NANOJ* 1(4): 289.

localized in the central and southern Appalachian Mountains, often around and under
Rhododendron maximum

Hybrid:

Listera ×*veltmanii* Case
Veltman's hybrid twayblade
(*L. auriculata* × *L. convallarioides*)

Macradenia lutescens R. Brown

Trinidad macradenia

southeastern Florida; West Indies, northern South America

formerly plentiful; perhaps extirpated at this time

Malaxis abieticola Salazar & Soto Arenas

 Malaxis tenuis (S. Watson) Ames C, L, P, W, F

fir-dwelling adder's-mouth

Arizona, New Mexico; Mexico
Salazar, G.A., and M.A. Soto Arenas. 2001. *Lindleyana* 16(3): 149.

one of the larger flowered species of the genus in the Southwest

Malaxis bayardii Fernald

Malaxis unifolia var. *bayardii nom. nud.*

Bayard's adder's-mouth

Nova Scotia; Massachusetts south to South Carolina, west to Ohio
Catling, P.M. 1991. *Lindleyana* 6(1): 3–23.

buried for many years within *M. unifolia,* this species is either very rare and local or easily overlooked

Malaxis brachypoda (Gray) Fernald

Malaxis monophyllos (Linnaeus) Swartz var. *brachypoda* (A. Gray) Morris & Eames C, L, P, W, F

white adder's-mouth

southern Alaska east to Newfoundland, south to California, Colorado, Indiana, Pennsylvania, and New England
   forma *bifolia* (Mousley) Fernald— two-leaved form

widely scattered throughout the range; locally common in western Newfoundland

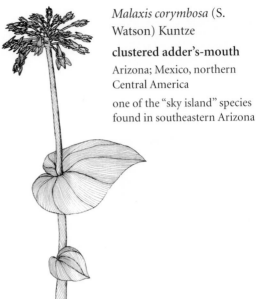

Malaxis corymbosa (S. Watson) Kuntze

clustered adder's-mouth

Arizona; Mexico, northern Central America

one of the "sky island" species found in southeastern Arizona

Malaxis diphyllos Chamisso

Malaxis monophyllos (Linnaeus) Swartz var. *diphyllos* (Chamisso) Luer L, W

Malaxis monophyllos (Linnaeus) Swartz var. *monophyllos* F

two-leaved adder's-mouth

southwestern Alaska, western British Columbia

rare and local on the Alaskan islands

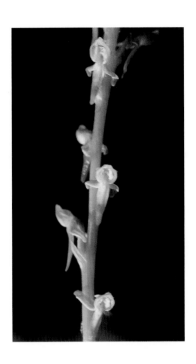

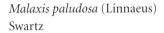

Malaxis paludosa (Linnaeus) Swartz

Hammarbya paludosa (Linnaeus) Kuntze

bog adder's-mouth

Alaska east to western Ontario, south to Minnesota; northern Eurasia

Reeves, T., and L.M. Reeves. 1984. *AOS Bulletin* 53(12): 1280–92.

———. 1985. *Rhodora* 87: 133–36.

rare and local throughout the range

Malaxis porphyrea (Ridley) Kuntze

Microstylis porphyrea Ridley

Malaxis ehrenbergii (Reichenbach *f.*) Kuntze misapplied C, L, P, W

Malaxis wendtii Salazar misapplied

purple adder's-mouth

Arizona, New Mexico; Mexico

Todsen, T. 1997. *Sida* 17: 637–38.

a Mexican species that crosses the border in the southwestern states

Malaxis soulei L.O. Williams

Malaxis macrostachys (Lexarza) Kuntze *nomen confusum* L, W

Malaxis montana (Rothrock) O. Kuntze

rat-tailed adder's-mouth

Arizona, New Mexico, and Texas; Mexico

the most widespread of the Mexican adder's-mouths in the United States

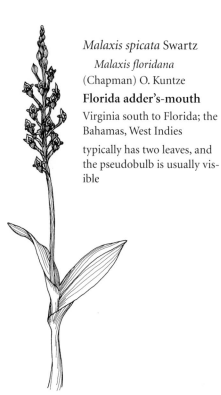

Malaxis spicata Swartz

Malaxis floridana (Chapman) O. Kuntze

Florida adder's-mouth

Virginia south to Florida; the Bahamas, West Indies

typically has two leaves, and the pseudobulb is usually visible

Malaxis unifolia Michaux

Microstylis unifolia (Michaux) Britton, Sterns, & Poggenberg

green adder's-mouth

Manitoba east to Newfoundland, south to Texas and east to Florida; West Indies, Mexico, northern Central America

forma *bifolia* Mousley—two-leaved form

forma *variegata* Mousley—variegated-leaf form

widespread in a variety of habitats; locally common in some areas

Malaxis wendtii Salazar

Wendt's adder's-mouth

southern Texas; Mexico

Salazar, G. 1993. *Orquidea* (Mexico City) 13(1–2): 281–84.

Todsen, T. 1995. *Sida* 16(3): 591.

———. 1997. *Sida* 17: 637–38.

known from only the Boot Spring area of Big Bend National Park, Texas

Maxillaria crassifolia (Lindley) Reichenbach f.

Maxillaria sessilis (Schweinfurth) Fawcett & Rendle

false butterfly orchid

southwestern Florida; West Indies, Mexico, Central America, northern South America

restricted to the Faka-hatchee/Big Cypress area of southwestern Florida

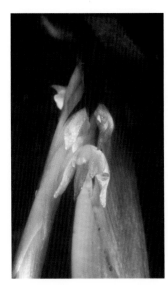

Maxillaria parviflora (Poeppig & Endlicher) Garay

Maxillaria conferta (Grisebach) C. Schweinfurth *ex* Leon
Maxillaria purpurea (Sprengel) Ames & Correll *p.p.*

densely-flowered maxillaria

southwestern Florida; West Indies, Mexico, Central America, South America

Atwood, J.T. 1993. *Lindleyana* 8(1): 25–31.
Hammer, R. 1981. *Fairchild Tropical Garden Bulletin* 36(3): 16–18.
McCartney, C. 1993. *Florida Orchidist* 36(3): 25–29.

discovered in the Fakahatchee Swamp, Florida, in 1975 and not seen again since the early 1990s

Mesadenus lucayanus (Britton) Schlechter

> *Ibidium lucayanum* Britton
> *Spiranthes lucayana* (Britton) Cogniaux
> *Mesadenus polyanthus* (Reichenbach f.)
> Schlechter misapplied
> *Spiranthes polyanthus* Reichenbach f. misapplied c, l, w

copper ladies'-tresses

Florida; Mexico, the Bahamas, West Indies, Central America
Brown, P.M. 2000. *NANOJ* 6(4): 335–36.

this rather inconspicuous species is known from only a few widely separated locales

Oeceoclades maculata
(Lindley) Lindley*

> *Eulophidium maculatum*
> (Lindley) Pfitzer

spotted African orchis

Florida; West Indies, Central America, South America, Africa
Johnson, S.R. 1993. *Lindleyana* 8(2): 69–72.
Stern, W.S. 1988. *AOS Bulletin* 57(9): 960–71.

a rapidly spreading African species that is throughout the Caribbean and parts of South America; first seen in Florida in 1974

Oncidium floridanum
Ames
   Oncidium ensatum
Lindley misapplied F
Florida oncidium
southern Florida; the Bahamas
a large, showy terrestrial that is scattered in southern Florida

Pelexia adnata (Swartz)
Sprengel
   Spiranthes adnata (Swartz)
Bentham *ex* Fawcett
glandular ladies'-tresses
southeastern Florida; West Indies, Central America, Mexico, northern South America
Hammer, R.L. 1981. *Fairchild Tropical Garden Bulletin* 36(3): 16–18.
McCartney, C.L., Jr. 1983. *Florida Orchidist* 26(3): 124–29.

first found in 1977 near Everglades National Park, Florida; by 1986 plants had completely disappeared; presumed extirpated

Phaius tankervilleae (Aiton) Blume*

Phaius grandifolia Lindley

nun orchid

central Florida; southeast Asia, Australia; naturalized in the West Indies
Brown, P.M. 2001. *NANOJ* 7(1): 96–97.

first vouchered report of a thoroughly naturalized colony was in 2001

Piperia candida Morgan & Ackerman

slender white piperia

southeastern Alaska south to California
Morgan, R., and J. Ackerman. 1990. *Lindleyana* 5(4): 205–11.

plants are similar to *P. unalascensis,* but flower color is distinctive

Piperia colemanii Morgan & Glicenstein

Coleman's piperia

California
Morgan, R., and L. Glicenstein. 1993. *Lindleyana* 8(2): 89–95.

another segregate from *P. unalascensis*, typified by the tiny spur

Piperia cooperi (S. Watson) Rydberg

Cooper's stout-spire orchid

California; Mexico
Coleman, R.A. 1992. *AOS Bulletin* 61(2): 130–35.
———. 1995. *NANOJ* 1(1): 75–78.

the southernmost ranging of the genus

Piperia elegans (Lindley) Rydberg subsp. *elegans*

    Habenaria elegans (Lindley) Bolander

    Habenaria elegans Jepson var. *maritima* (Greene) Ames

    Habenaria greenei Jepson

    Habenaria maritima Greene

    Habenaria unalascensis (Sprengel) S. Watson var. *maritima* (Greene) Correll c

    Piperia maritima (Greene) Rydberg l, p, w

    Piperia multiflora Rydberg

    Platanthera unalascensis (Sprengel) Rydberg subsp. *maritima* (Greene) de Filipps

    Platanthera unalascensis (Sprengel) Rydberg var. *maritima* (Greene) Correll

elegant piperia

British Columbia south to California; northern Idaho, western Montana

widespread and striking with its large, snow-white flowers

Piperia elegans (Lindley) Rydberg subsp. *decurtata* Morgan & Glicenstein

Point Reyes piperia

west-central California

Morgan, R., and L. Glicenstein. 1993. *Lindleyana* 8(2): 89–95.

an endemic to the Point Reyes area north of San Francisco, California

Piperia elongata Rydberg

Habenaria unalascensis (Sprengel) S. Watson subsp. *elata* (Jepson) Calder

Habenaria unalascensis (Sprengel) S. Watson var. *elata* (Jepson) Correll c

Piperia elegans (Lindley) Rydberg var. *elata* (Jepson) Luer l

Piperia lancifolia Rydberg

Piperia longispica (Durand) Rydberg

Platanthera unalascensis (Sprengel) Rydberg subsp. *elata* (Jepson) Taylor & MacBryde

long-spurred piperia

British Columbia south to California; northern Idaho and western Montana

the distinctive elongated spur is diagnostic in this species

Piperia leptopetala Rydberg

lace orchid

California

recognized by its very delicate and slender flowers; unvouchered reports for Oregon and Washington

Piperia michaelii (E. Greene)
Rydberg

> *Habenaria michaelii* Greene
> *Piperia elongata* Rydberg var.
> *michaelii* (Greene) Ackerman

Michael's piperia

Oregon south to California

primarily a coastal species

Piperia transversa Suksdorf

flat-spurred piperia

British Columbia south
to California

the straight, transverse
spur helps separate this
from *P. elongata*

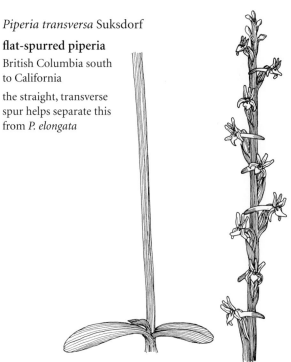

Piperia unalascensis (Sprengel) Rydberg

Habenaria unalascensis (Sprengel) S. Watson C
Platanthera unalascensis (Sprengel) Kurtz
Spiranthes unalascensis Sprengel

Alaskan piperia

Alaska south to California, Montana, northern New Mexico, east to Ontario, Michigan, Quebec, Newfoundland

the most widespread and most frequently encountered of the genus

Piperia yadonii R. Morgan & J. Ackerman

Yadon's piperia

California
Morgan, R., and J. Ackerman. 1990.
  Lindleyana 5(4): 205–11.

federally listed as endangered; endemic to the Monterey Peninsula, California

Platanthera aquilonis Sheviak

Habenaria hyperborea (Linnaeus) R. Brown *ex* Aiton misapplied C

Platanthera hyperborea (Linnaeus) Lindley misapplied L, P, W

northern green bog orchis

Alaska east to Newfoundland, south to New Mexico and Iowa, east to Massachusetts

forma *alba* (Light) P.M. Brown—albino form

Brown, P.M. 2000. *NANOJ* 6(1): 43.

Light, M.S., and M. MacConaill. 1989. *Lindleyana* 4(3): 158–60.

Sheviak, C.J. 1999. *Lindleyana* 14(4): 193–203.

plants in North America (excepting Greenland) were formerly known as *P. hyperborea*

Platanthera blephariglottis (Willdenow) Lindley var. *blephariglottis*

Blephariglottis blephariglottis (Willdenow) Rydberg

Habenaria blephariglottis (Willdenow) Hooker C

northern white fringed orchis

Michigan east to Newfoundland, south to Georgia

forma *holopetala* (Lindley) P.M. Brown—entire-lip form

Brown, P.M. 1988. *Wild Flower Notes* 3(1): 20.

widespread and often locally abundant in a variety of damp to wet habitats

Platanthera blephariglottis
(Willdenow) Lindley var. *conspicua*
(Nash) Luer

Blephariglottis conspicua (Nash)
Small
Habenaria blephariglottis
(Willdenow) Hooker var. *conspicua*
(Nash) Ames c
Habenaria conspicua Nash

southern white fringed orchis

North Carolina south to Florida,
west to Texas

the southern counterpart to variety
blephariglottis, but quite distinct in
several characters

Platanthera brevifolia (Greene) Kranzlein

Habenaria brevifolia Greene
Habenaria sparsiflora S. Watson var. *brevifolia*
(Greene) Correll c
Limnorchis brevifolia (Greene) Rydberg
Platanthera sparsiflora (S. Watson)
Schlechter var. *brevifolia* (Greene) Luer L, W

**short-leaved rein
orchis**

New Mexico;
Mexico

vegetatively dis-
tinctive; leaves are
so short on some
plants that the
plants may appear
not to have any
leaves

Platanthera chapmanii (Small) Luer
emend. Folsom

> *Blephariglottis chapmanii* Small
> *Habenaria ×chapmanii* (Small) Ames c
> *Platanthera ×chapmanii* (Small) Luer L

Chapman's fringed orchis

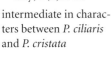

southeastern Georgia, northern Florida, and eastern Texas
Folsom, J.P. 1984.
> *Orquidea* (Mexico City) 9(2): 344.

intermediate in characters between *P. ciliaris* and *P. cristata*

Platanthera chorisiana
(Chamisso) Reichenbach *f.*
> *Habenaria chorisiana* Chamisso c
> *Limnorchis chorisiana* (Chamisso)

J.P. Anderson
> *Pseudodiphryllum chorisianum*
(Chamisso) Nevski

Chamisso's orchid

Alaska south to northern Washington; Asia

very rare to local in scattered sites

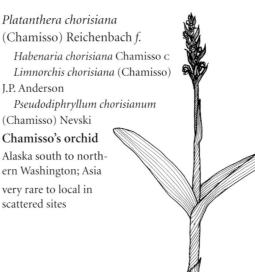

Platanthera ciliaris (Linnaeus) Lindley

  Habenaria ciliaris (Linnaeus) R. Brown *ex* Aiton c

orange fringed orchis

Michigan east to Massachusetts, south to Texas and Florida

one of the showiest of all of our native orchids

Platanthera clavellata (Michaux) Luer var. *clavellata*

  Gymnadeniopsis clavellata (Michaux) Rydberg
  Habenaria clavellata (Michaux) Sprengel c

little club-spur orchis

Wisconsin east to Maine, south to Texas and Georgia
  forma *slaughteri* P.M. Brown—white-flowered form Brown, P.M. 1995. *NANOJ* 1(3): 200.

an often frequent orchid in both sunny and shady wet habitats, especially in disturbed areas

Platanthera clavellata (Michaux) Luer var. *ophioglossoides* (Fernald) P.M. Brown

Gymnadeniopsis clavellata (Michaux) Rydberg var. *ophioglossoides* (Fernald) Schrenk

Habenaria clavellata (Michaux) Sprengel var. *ophioglossoides* Fernald c

northern club-spur orchis

Ontario east to Newfoundland, south to Michigan and Massachusetts

Brown, P.M. 1988. *Wild Flower Notes* 3(1): 21.

differing from the nominate variety by its northerly distribution, single large basal leaf, and congested inflorescence

Platanthera cristata (Michaux) Lindley

Habenaria cristata (Michaux) R. Brown c

orange crested orchis

Massachusetts south to Florida, west to Texas

forma *straminea* P.M. Brown— pale yellow-flowered form

Brown, P.M. 1995. *NANOJ* 1(1): 12.

locally frequent on the central and southern coastal plain

Platanthera dilatata (Pursh) Lindley var. *dilatata*

 Habenaria dilatata (Pursh) Hooker c
 Limnorchis dilatata (Pursh) Rydberg *ex* Britton

tall white northern bog orchis

Alaska east to Newfoundland, south to Washington and New Mexico; Minnesota south to Indiana, Pennsylvania, and New England

widespread throughout the northern portion of the continent; intense, spicy fragrance

Platanthera dilatata (Pursh) Lindley var. *albiflora* (Chamisso) Ledebour

 Habenaria borealis Chamisso var. *albiflora* Chamisso
 Habenaria dilatata (Pursh) Hooker var. *albiflora* (Chamisso) Correll c

bog candles

Alaska south to Oregon, east to Utah and Colorado

the most frequently seen variety in the Pacific Northwest

Platanthera dilatata (Pursh) Lindley var. *leucostachys* (Lindley) Luer

   Habenaria dilatata (Pursh) Hooker var. *leucostachys* (Lindley) Ames c
   Habenaria leucostachys (Lindley) S. Watson
   Limnorchis leucostachys (Lindley) Rydberg
   Platanthera leucostachys Lindley

Sierra rein-orchid

southern Alaska south to California, east to Wyoming and Utah

the largest and showiest of the three varieties

Platanthera flava (Linnaeus) Lindley var. *flava*

   Habenaria flava (Linnaeus) R. Brown *ex* Sprengel c

southern tubercled orchis

southern Nova Scotia, southern Ontario; Missouri east to Maryland, south to Texas and Florida

found in both woodlands and open roadsides as well as pond shores

Platanthera flava (Linnaeus) Lindley var. *herbiola* (R. Brown) Luer

Habenaria flava (Linnaeus) R. Brown var. *herbiola* (R. Brown *ex* Aiton) Ames & Correll c
  Habenaria flava var. *virescens sensu* Fernald
  Habenaria herbiola R. Brown *ex* Aiton

northern tubercled orchis

Minnesota east to Nova Scotia, south to Missouri and Georgia; south in the Appalachian Mts.
  forma *lutea* (Boivin) Whiting & Catling—yellow-flowered form

has a sweet fragrance and the distinctive tubercle on the lip; often found in seasonally flooded areas, grassy meadows, and red maple floodplains

Platanthera grandiflora (Bigelow) Lindley

Blephariglottis grandiflora (Bigelow) Rydberg
  Habenaria fimbriata (Dryander) R. Brown *ex* Aiton
  Habenaria grandiflora (Bigelow) Torrey
  Habenaria psycodes (Linnaeus) Sprengel var. *grandiflora* (Bigelow) A. Gray c

large purple fringed orchis

Ontario east to Newfoundland, south to West Virginia and New Jersey; south in the Appalachian Mts. to Georgia
  forma *albiflora* (Rand & Redfield) Catling—white-flowered form
  forma *bicolor* P.M. Brown—bicolor-flowered form
  forma *carnea* P.M. Brown—pink-flowered form
  forma *mentotonsa* (Fernald) P.M. Brown—entire-lip form
Brown, P.M. 1988. *Wild Flower Notes* 3(1): 22.
  ———. 1995. *NANOJ* 1(1): 12.
Stoutamire, W.P. 1974. *Brittonia* 26: 42–58.

highly variable in color; habit is affected by habitat—plants of deep shade are tall and stately while those in full sun may be stout and full

Platanthera hookeri (Torrey) Lindley

> *Habenaria hookeri* Torrey C

Hooker's orchis

Manitoba east to Newfoundland, south to Iowa and New Jersey

> forma *abbreviata* (Fernald) P.M. Brown—dwarfed form
>
> Brown, P.M. 1995. *NANOJ* 1(1): 14.

rich woods in widely scattered locales, with flowers that look like ice tongs or gargoyles!

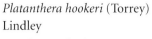

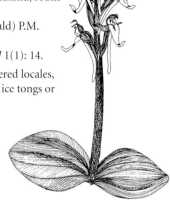

Platanthera huronensis (Nuttall) Lindley

> *Habenaria hyperborea* (Linnaeus) R. Brown *ex* Aiton var. *huronensis* (Nuttall) Farwell C
>
> *Habenaria* ×*media* (Rydberg) Niles
> *Limnorchis media* Rydberg
> *Platanthera hyperborea* (Linnaeus) Lindley var. *huronensis* (Nuttall) Luer L, W
>
> *Platanthera* ×*media* (Rydberg) Luer

green bog orchis

Alaska east to Newfoundland, south to New Mexico and Pennsylvania

the most widespread and frequently encountered of all of the green-flowered rein orchids

Platanthera hyperborea (Linnaeus) Lindley

Habenaria hyperborea (Linnaeus) R. Brown *ex* Aiton c
Limnorchis hyperborea (Linnaeus) Rydberg

northern rein orchis

Greenland; Iceland
Sheviak, C.J. 1999. *Lindleyana*
14(4): 193–203.

included in the flora based
upon its occurrence in
Greenland; plants previ-
ously known as this spe-
cies elsewhere in North
America are now known
as *P. aquilonis*

Platanthera integra (Nuttall) Lindley

Gymnadeniopsis integra (Nuttall) Rydberg
Habenaria integra (Nuttall) Sprengel c

yellow fringeless orchis

New Jersey south to Florida, west
to Texas

rare and local in most areas;
populations are declining due
to loss of habitat

Platanthera integrilabia (Correll) Luer

Habenaria blephariglottis (Willdenow) Hooker var. *integrilabia* Correll c

Habenaria correlliana Cronquist

monkey-face orchis

Kentucky and North Carolina, south to Mississippi and Georgia

Zettler, L.W. 1994. *AOS Bulletin* 63(6): 686–88.

Zettler, L.W., and J.E. Fairey, III. 1992. *Lindleyana* (4): 212–17.

one of the most restricted of all *Platanthera* species, known from only a few sites in each state

Platanthera lacera (Michaux) G. Don

Habenaria lacera (Michaux) R. Brown c

green fringed orchis, ragged orchis

Manitoba east to Newfoundland, south to Texas and Georgia

Catling, P.M. 1997. *Lindleyana* 12(2): 79–88.

roadsides, haymeadows, and fields accommodate this common and widespread species

Platanthera leucophaea (Nuttall) Lindley

Habenaria leucophaea (Nuttall) A. Gray c

eastern prairie fringed orchis

Nebraska east to Ontario and Maine, south to Oklahoma and Virginia

Sheviak, C.J., and M. Bowles. 1986. *Rhodora* 88: 267–90.

federally listed as threatened, this fragrant beauty has but a few strongholds left

Platanthera limosa Lindley

Habenaria limosa (Lindley) Hemsley c

Habenaria thurberi A. Gray

Limnorchis arizonica Rydberg

Thurber's bog orchid

Arizona and New Mexico; Mexico

occurs in local populations at higher elevations

Platanthera macrophylla (Goldie) P.M. Brown

> *Habenaria macrophylla* Goldie
> *Platanthera orbiculata* var. *macrophylla* (Goldie) Luer L, w

Goldie's pad-leaved orchis

Ontario east to Newfoundland, south to Michigan and Pennsylvania

Brown, P.M. 1988. *Wild Flower Notes* 3(1): 23.

Reddoch, A.H., and J.M. Reddoch 1993. *Lindleyana* 8(4): 171–88.

rich, damp mixed woodlands; populations can vary from single individuals to several hundred

Platanthera nivea (Nuttall) Luer

> *Gymnadeniopsis nivea* (Nuttall) Rydberg
> *Habenaria nivea* (Nuttall) Sprengel C

snowy orchis

southern New Jersey south to Florida, west to Texas

fragrant and elegant; the non-resupinate lip differentiates this species from any other *Platanthera*

Platanthera obtusata (Banks *ex* Pursh) Lindley
subsp. *obtusata*

   Habenaria obtusata (Banks *ex* Pursh) Richards c

blunt-leaved rein orchis

Alaska east to Newfoundland, south to
Colorado, upper Great Lakes region and
east to western Massachusetts
   forma *collectanea* (Fernald) P.M.
Brown—dwarfed form
   forma *foliosa* P.M. Brown—multiple-
leaved form
Brown, P.M. 1995. *NANOJ* 1(1): 13–14.

the typical single leaf is unique among
our species of *Platanthera*

Platanthera obtusata (Banks *ex*
Pursh) Lindley subsp. *oligantha*
(Turczaninow) Hultén

   Habenaria obtusata (Banks *ex* Pursh)
Richards var. *oligantha* (Turczaninow)
B. Boivin
    Platanthera oligantha Turczaninow
    Platanthera parvula Schlechter

**few-flowered blunt-leaved rein
orchis**

northern Alaska; northern Eurasia
Hultén, E. 1968. *Flora of Alaska*, p. 325.
Sheviak, C.J. 2002. *FNA*, vol. 26, p. 556.

known only from a few collections in
Alaska; very rare in Eurasia

Platanthera orbiculata (Pursh) Lindley

Habenaria orbiculata (Pursh) Torrey c

Habenaria orbiculata (Pursh) Torrey var. *menziesii* (Lindley) Fernald

pad-leaved orchis

southeastern Alaska, British Columbia east to Newfoundland, south to northern Oregon and Maryland, south in the Appalachian Mts. to North Carolina

forma *lehorsii* (Fernald) P.M. Brown— dwarfed form

forma *trifolia* (Mousley) P.M. Brown— three-leaved form

Brown, P.M. 1995. *NANOJ* 1(1): 15.
Reddoch, A.H., and J.M. Reddoch. 1993. *Lindleyana* 8(4): 171–88.

more widespread than *P. macrophylla*, with which it is often confused

Platanthera pallida P.M. Brown

pale fringed orchis

eastern New York
Brown, P.M. 1993. *Novon* 2(4): 308–11.

endemic to eastern Long Island; plants are closely akin to *P. cristata* and treated by some authors as synonymous

Platanthera peramoena
(A. Gray) A. Gray

*Blephariglottis
peramoena* (Gray) Rydberg
Habenaria peramoena A.
Gray c

purple fringeless orchis

Missouri east to New Jersey, south to Mississippi
and Georgia

Spooner, D.M., and J.S.
Shelly. 1983. *Rhodora* 85:
55–64.

one of the tallest species of
Platanthera, often reaching
a meter in height

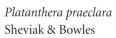

Platanthera praeclara
Sheviak & Bowles

Habenaria leucophaea
(Nuttall) A. Gray var.
praeclara (Sheviak & Bowles)
Cronquist

**western prairie fringed
orchis**

federally listed as threatened;
Wyoming east to southern
Manitoba, south to Oklahoma and Missouri

Sheviak, C.J., and M. Bowles.
1986. *Rhodora* 88: 267–90.

a grandiose counterpart to
the eastern *P. leucophaea;* the
largest individual flowers of
any species within the fringed
orchis group

Platanthera psycodes (Linnaeus) Lindley

Blephariglottis psycodes (Linnaeus) Rydberg

Habenaria psycodes (Linnaeus) Sprengel c

small purple fringed orchis

Manitoba east to Newfoundland, south to Ohio and New Jersey, south in the Appalachian Mts. to Georgia

forma *albiflora* (R. Hoffman) Whiting & Catling—white-flowered form

forma *ecalcarata* (Bryan) P.M. Brown—spurless form

forma *rosea* P.M. Brown—pink-flowered form

forma *varians* (Bryan) P.M. Brown—entire-lip form

Brown, P.M. 1988. *Wild Flower Notes* 3(1): 24.

———.1995. *NANOJ* 1(4): 289.

Stoutamire, W.P. 1974. *Brittonia* 26: 42–58.

not necessarily "smaller" than *P. grandiflora*, but usually with smaller individual flowers and different nectary shape

Platanthera purpurascens (Rydberg) Sheviak & Jennings

Habenaria hyperborea (Linnaeus) R. Brown var. *purpurascens* (Rydberg) Ames c

Limnorchis purpurascens Rydberg

Platanthera hyperborea (Linnaeus) Lindley var. *purpurascens* (Rydberg) Luer L, w

short-spurred bog orchis

California; Arizona east to New Mexico, and north to southern Wyoming

Sheviak, C.J., and W. Jennings. 1997. *NANOJ* 3(4): 444–49.

restricted distribution and not well understood; somewhat variable in coloring

Platanthera sparsiflora (S. Watson)
Schlechter var. *sparsiflora*

   Habenaria sparsiflora S. Watson c
   Habenaria sparsiflora S. Watson var. *laxiflora*
(Rydberg) Correll
     Limnorchis ensifolia Rydberg
     Limnorchis laxiflora Rydberg
     Limnorchis sparsiflora (S. Watson) Rydberg
     Platanthera sparsiflora (S. Watson) Schlechter
var. *ensifolia* (Rydberg) Luer

few-flowered rein-orchis

Oregon south to California, east to Utah, New
Mexico; Mexico

highly variable; environment affects habit

Platanthera stricta Lindley

   Habenaria borealis Chamisso var. *viridiflora*
Chamisso
     Habenaria saccata Greene c
     Limnorchis stricta (Lindley) Rydberg
     Platanthera gracilis Lindley
     Platanthera hyperborea var. *viridiflora*
(Chamisso) Kitamura
     Platanthera hyperborea
var. *viridiflora* (Chamisso)
Luer
     Platanthera saccata
(Greene) Hultén

slender bog orchis

Alaska east to Alberta,
south to California and
Wyoming

exceedingly variable,
but most plants have
the diagnostic
scrotiform spur

Platanthera tipuloides (Linnaeus)
Lindley var. *behringiana*
(Rydberg) Hultén

> *Habenaria behringiana* (Rydberg)
> Ames c
> *Limnorchis behringiana* Rydberg

Behring orchid

Alaska; northeastern Asia

restricted to the outer Aleutian Islands

Platanthera zothecina (Higgins & Welsh)
Kartesz & Gandhi

> *Habenaria zothecina* Higgins & Welsh

cloistered bog orchid

Utah, Colorado, Arizona

Higgins, L.C., and S.L. Welsh. 1986. *Great Basin Naturalist* 46: 259.

Hudson, L.E., R.A. Coleman, and S. Charles. 2000. *NANOJ* 6(2): 103–18.

the leaves are all clustered near the base of the stem; flowers unusually long-spurred for this group

note:

Platanthera convallariaefolia (Fischer) Lindley, **lily-leaved rein orchis,** is included in the flora based upon a few collections from the outer Aleutian Islands that may be this species; these specimens are not conclusive and should not be confused with plants often illustrated as this species (or variety) in several works.

Hybrids:

Platanthera ×andrewsii (Niles) Luer

    Platanthera lacera (Michaux) G. Don var. *terrae-novae* (Fernald) Luer L

        Habenaria ×andrewsii Niles

        Habenaria lacera (Michaux) R. Brown var. *terrae-novae* Fernald C

Andrews' hybrid fringed orchis

(*P. lacera* × *P. psycodes*)

Catling, P.M., and V. Catling. 1994. *Lindleyana* 9(1): 19–32.

Platanthera ×bicolor (Rafinesque) Luer

    Habenaria ×bicolor Rafinesque

bicolor hybrid fringed orchis

(*P. blephariglottis* × *P. ciliaris*)

Platanthera ×canbyi (Ames) Luer

    Habenaria ×canbyi Ames C

Canby's hybrid fringed orchis

(*P. blephariglottis* × *P. cristata*)

Platanthera ×channellii Folsom

Channell's hybrid fringed orchis

(*P. ciliaris* × *P. cristata*)

Folsom, J.P. 1984. *Orquidea* (Mexico City) 9(2): 344.

Platanthera ×correllii Schrenck

Correll's hybrid rein orchis

(*P. aquilonis* × *P. stricta*)

Schrenck, W.J. 1975. *Die Orchidee* 26: 258–63.

———.1978. *AOS Bulletin* 47(5): 429–37.

Platanthera ×estesii Schrenck

Estes hybrid rein orchis

(*P. dilatata* var. *albiflora* × *P. stricta*)

Schrenck, W.J. 1975. *Die Orchidee* 26: 258–63.

———. 1978. *AOS Bulletin* 47(5): 429–37.

Platanthera ×hollandiae Catling & Brownell

Holland River hybrid fringed orchis

(*P. leucophaea* × *P. lacera*)

Catling, P.M. and V. Brownell. 1999. *Canadian Journal of Botany* 77(8): 1144-49.

Platanthera ×keenanii P.M. Brown

Keenan's hybrid fringed orchis

(*P. grandiflora* × *P. lacera*)

Brown, P.M. 1993. *A Field Guide to the Orchids of New England and New York,* p. 189.

Catling, P.M., and V. Catling. 1994. *Lindleyana* 9(1): 19–32.

Platanthera ×lassenii Schrenk

Lassen hybrid rein orchis

(*P. dilatata* var. *leucostachys* × *P. sparsiflora*)

Schrenck, W.J. 1975. *Die Orchidee* 26: 258–63.

———. 1978. *AOS Bulletin* 47(5): 429–37.

Platanthera ×reznicekii Catling, Brownell, & G. Allen

Reznicek's hybrid fringed orchid

(*P. leucophaea* × *P. psycodes*)

Catling, P.M., V. Brownell, and G. Allen. 1999. *Lindleyana* 14(2): 77–86.

Platanthera ×vossii Case

Voss' hybrid rein orchis

(*P. blephariglottis* × *P. clavellata* var. *ophioglossoides*)

Case, F.W. 1983. *Michigan Botanist* 22: 141–44.

Platythelys querceticola (Lindley)
Garay

> *Erythrodes querceticola* (Lindley)
Ames c, l, w
> > *Physurus querceticola* Lindley

low ground orchid, jug orchid
Louisiana east to Florida

widely scattered; populations tend
to be very local

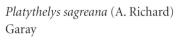

Platythelys sagreana (A. Richard)
Garay

> *Erythrodes querceticola* Lindley var.
sagreana (A. Richard) Small l
> > *Erythrodes sagreana* (A. Richard) Leon
> > *Physurus sagraeanus* A. Richard

Cuban ground orchid
southern Florida; West Indies
Brown, P.M. 1998. *NANOJ* 5(1): 3.

found in the southern third of Florida

Pleurothallis gelida Lindley

Stelis gelida (Lindley) Pridgeon & M.W. Chase

frosted pleurothallis

southern Florida; West Indies, Central America, South America

Pridgeon, A.M., and M.W. Chase. 2001. *Lindleyana* 16(4): 235–71.

restricted to the Fakahatchee Swamp and environs in southwestern Florida

Pogonia ophioglossoides (Linnaeus) Ker-Gawler

rose pogonia

Manitoba east to Newfoundland, south to Texas and Florida

forma *albiflora* Rand & Redfield—white-flowered form

forma *brachypogon* (Fernald) P.M. Brown—short-bearded form

Brown, P.M. 1998. *NANOJ* 6(4): 339.

one of the most widely distributed orchids in eastern North America

Polystachya concreta (Jacquin) Garay & Sweet

Polystachya flavescens (Lindley) J.J. Small ʟ

Polystachya luteola (Swartz) Hooker *nom. illeg.*
c, w

Polystachya minuta (Aublet) Britton *nom. illeg.*

pale-flowered polystachya

southern Florida; West
Indies, northern and cen-
tral South America

the characteristic one-
sided, branched
racemes are unlike
any other epi-
phytic orchid in
North America

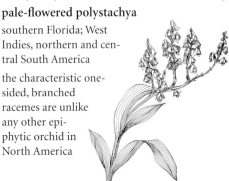

Ponthieva brittoniae Ames

Ponthieva racemosa (Walter) C. Mohr var. *brittonae* (Ames) Luer ʟ

Mrs. Britton's shadow-witch

southeastern Florida; the Bahamas
McCartney, C.L., Jr. 1995. *NANOJ*
1(2): 106–16.

known from
Everglades National
Park, Florida;
possibly extirpated

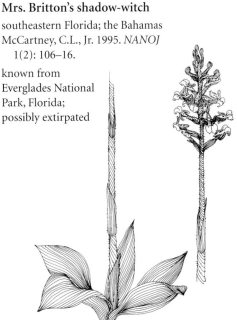

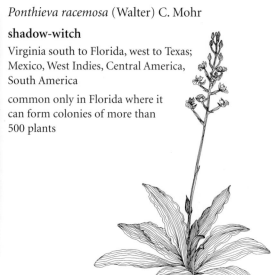

Ponthieva racemosa (Walter) C. Mohr

shadow-witch

Virginia south to Florida, west to Texas; Mexico, West Indies, Central America, South America

common only in Florida where it can form colonies of more than 500 plants

Prescottia oligantha (Swartz) Lindley

small prescottia

southern Florida; West Indies, Central America, northern and central South America

a delicate cousin to *Spiranthes,* not seen since Hurricane Andrew in 1992

Prosthechea boothiana (Lindley) W.E. Higgins var. *erythronioides* (Small) W.E. Higgins

Encyclia boothiana (Lindley) Dressler var. *erythronioides* (Small) Luer L, W

Epidendrum boothianum Lindley C

Epidendrum erythronioides Small

Prosthechea boothiana (Lindley) W.E. Higgins subsp. *erythronioides* (Small) Nir

Florida dollar orchid

southern Florida; Central America, West Indies

Brown, P.M. 1998. *NANOJ* 4(1): 52.

Higgins, W.E. 1998. *Phytologia* 85(5): 370–83.

pseudobulbs are round and flat like silver dollars, hence the common name

Prosthechea cochleata (Linnaeus) W.E. Higgins var. *triandra* (Ames) W.E. Higgins

Anacheilum cochleatum (Linnaeus) Hoffmannsegg var. *triandrum* (Ames) Sauleda, Wunderlin, & Hansen

Encyclia cochleata (Linnaeus) Dressler subsp. *triandra* (Ames) Hágsater

Encyclia cochleata (Linnaeus) Dressler var. *triandra* (Ames) Dressler L, W

Epidendrum cochleatum Linnaeus subsp. *triandrum* Ames

Epidendrum cochleatum Linnaeus var. *triandrum* Ames C

Prosthechea cochleata (Linnaeus) W.E. Higgins subsp. *triandra* (Ames) Nir

Florida clamshell orchid

southern Florida; (West Indies?)

forma *albidoflava* (P.M. Brown) P.M. Brown—pale-colored form

Brown, P.M. 1995. *NANOJ* 1(2): 131.

———. 1998. *NANOJ* 4(1): 53.

Higgins, W.E. 1998. *Phytologia* 85(5): 370–83.

one of the most popular and distinctive of our natives; widespread in southern Florida

Prosthechea pygmaea (Hooker) W.E. Higgins

Encyclia pygmaea (Hooker) Dressler L, W
Epidendrum pygmaeum Hooker C
Hormidium pygmaeum (Hooker) Bentham &
Hooker *ex* Hemsley

dwarf butterfly orchid

southwestern Florida; West Indies, Mexico, Central America, northern South America
Brown, P.M. 1998. *NANOJ* 4(1): 52.
Higgins, W.E. 1998. *Phytologia* 85(5): 370–83.

the tiniest of this group, and restricted to a few trees in the Fakahatchee Swamp, Florida

Pseudorchis straminea (Fernald) Soo

Gymnadenia albida (Linnaeus) subsp. *straminea* (Fernald) B. Ljtnant
Habenaria albida (Linnaeus) R. Brown var. *straminea* (Fernald) Morris & Eames C
Habenaria straminea Fernald
Leucorchis albida (Linnaeus) E. Meyer *ex* Schur subsp. *straminea* (Fernald) A. Löve
Platanthera albida (Linnaeus) Lindley var. *straminea* (Fernald) Luer L, P, W
Pseudorchis albida (Linnaeus) Löve & Löve subsp. *straminea* (Fernald) Löve & Löve F

Newfoundland orchis

western Quebec, northwestern Newfoundland, Greenland; Iceland, northern Europe
Reinhammar, L. 1995. *Nordic Journal of Botany* 15(5): 469–81.
———. 1997. *NANOJ* 3(4): 407–25.

although greatly restricted in range, it can be locally abundant in northwestern Newfoundland

Pteroglossaspis ecristata (Fernald) Rolfe

Eulophia ecristata (Fernald) Ames C, L, W

crestless plume orchid

North Carolina south to Florida, west to Louisiana; Cuba, Colombia

forma *flava* P.M. Brown—yellow-flowered form

Brown, P.M. 2000. *NANOJ* 6(1): 64.

these plants look like black and yellow orchids on a stick

Sacoila lanceolata (Aublet) Garay var. *lanceolata*

Spiranthes lanceolata (Aublet) Leon L, W

Spiranthes orchioides (Swartz) A. Richard C

Stenorrhynchos lanceolatum (Aublet) Richard *ex* Sprengel

Stenorrhynchos orchioides (Swartz) L.C. Richard

leafless beaked orchid

Florida; Mexico, the Bahamas, West Indies, Central America, South America

forma *albidaviridis* Catling & Sheviak—white/green-flowered form

forma *folsomii* P.M. Brown—golden-bronze-flowered form

Brown, P.M. 1999. *NANOJ* 5(2): 169–73.

Catling, P.M., and C.J. Sheviak. 1993. *Lindleyana* 8(2): 77–81.

the most striking of all of the roadside orchids in central and southern Florida

Sacoila lanceolata (Aublet) Garay var. *paludicola* (Luer) Sauleda, Wunderlin, & Hansen

   Spiranthes lanceolata (Aublet) Leon var. *paludicola* Luer L

Fakahatchee beaked orchid

southern Florida
   forma *aurea* P.M. Brown—golden-yellow-flowered form
Brown, P.M. 2001. *NANOJ* 7(1): 95–96.
Catling, P.M., and C.J. Sheviak. 1993.
   Lindleyana 8(2): 77–81.

originally restricted to the Fakahatchee/ Big Cypress/Corkscrew Swamp areas of Collier County, Florida; several possibly introduced populations have recently been found in nearby county parks

Sacoila squamulosa (Kunth) Garay

   Sacoila lanceolata (Aublet) Garay var. *squamulosa* (Kunth) Szlachetko
   Spiranthes squamulosa (Kunth) Leon
   Stenorrhynchos squamulosum (Kunth) Sprengel

hoary leafless beaked orchid

Florida; West Indies, northern South America
Brown, P.M. 2000. *NANOJ* 6(4): 333–38.

easily separated from the similar *S. lanceolata* by the hoary dots on the stem and flowers; currently known from a single population in central Florida

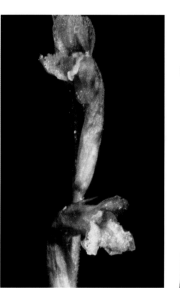

Schiedeella arizonica P.M. Brown

Schiedeella fauci-sanguinea (Dod) Burns-Balogh misapplied

Schiedeella parasitica (A. Richard & Galeotti) Schlechter misapplied

Spiranthes fauci-sanguinea Dod misapplied

Spiranthes parasitica A. Richard & Galeotti misapplied c, l, p, w

red-spot ladies'-tresses

Arizona east to western Texas
Brown, P.M. 1996. *NANOJ* 2(1): 66–68.
———. 2000. *NANOJ* 6(1): 3–17.

unlike any other spiranthoid species we have in North America; leaves not present at flowering time

Spathoglottis plicata Blume*

purple Javanese orchid

east-central Florida; Java, Asia, Pacific Islands, naturalized many other places including the West Indies
Brown, P.M. 2001. *NANOJ* 7(1): 96–97.

thoroughly naturalized in abandoned shellpits near West Palm Beach, Florida

Spiranthes amesiana Schlechter
emend. P.M. Brown

Ames' ladies'-tresses

southern Florida; the Bahamas,
Central America
Brown, P.M. *NANOJ* 7(1): 91–92.

overlooked; extirpated?

Spiranthes brevilabris Lindley

  Spiranthes gracilis (Bigelow) Beck var.
brevilabris (Lindley) Correll c

**short-lipped ladies'-tresses, Texas
ladies'-tresses**

Texas east to Georgia and Florida

only one extant site found in recent
years

Spiranthes casei Catling & Cruise var. *casei*

Spiranthes intermedia Ames misapplied ʟ

Case's ladies'-tresses

Ontario east to Nova Scotia, south to Wisconsin, northern Pennsylvania, and western Maine
Catling, P.M., and J.E. Cruise. 1974. *Rhodora* 76: 526–36.

widespread and scattered, primarily on the Canadian Shield

Spiranthes casei Catling & Cruise var. *novaescotiae* Catling

Case's Nova Scotian ladies'-tresses

Nova Scotia
Catling, P.M. 1981. *Canadian Journal of Botany* 59: 1253–70.

endemic to southern Nova Scotia

Spiranthes cernua (Linnaeus) L.C. Richard

Ibidium cernuum (Linnaeus) House

nodding ladies'-tresses

South Dakota east to Nova Scotia, south to Texas and Georgia

Sheviak, C.J. 1991. *Lindleyana* 6(4): 228–34.

a compilospecies throughout all of eastern North America (excluding Florida)

Spiranthes delitescens Sheviak

Spiranthes graminea Lindley misapplied L, P, W

Canelo Hills ladies'-tresses

Arizona

McClaren, M.C. 1996. *NANOJ* 2(2): 151–69.

McClaren, M.C., and P.C. Sundt. 1992. *Southwestern Naturalist* 37: 299–333.

Sheviak, C.J. 1990. *Rhodora* 92: 213–31.

federally listed as endangered; endemic to southwestern Arizona

Spiranthes diluvialis Sheviak

Spiranthes romanzoffiana Chamisso var. *diluvialis* (Sheviak) S.L. Welsh

Ute ladies'-tresses

northern Washington east to Wyoming, Montana, Nebraska, south to Nevada and Colorado

Arf, A.M. 1994. *Aquilegia* 18(2): 1, 4–5.
———. 1995. *NANOJ* 1(2): 117–28.
Sheviak, C.J. 1984. *Brittonia* 36: 8–14.

federally listed as threatened; an amphidiploid hybrid of *S. romanzoffiana* and *S. magnicamporum;* found in widely scattered areas

Spiranthes eatonii Ames *ex* P.M. Brown

Eaton's ladies'-tresses

southeast Virginia south to Florida, west to eastern Texas

Brown, P.M. 1999. *NANOJ* 5(1): 3.

the only white-flowered, basal rosetted *Spiranthes* to flower in the spring in North America

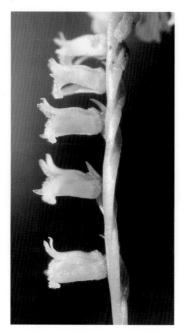

Spiranthes floridana (Wherry) Cory emend. P.M. Brown

> *Ibidium floridanum* Wherry
> *Spiranthes brevilabris* Lindley var.
> *floridana* (Wherry) Luer ʟ, w
> > *Spiranthes gracilis* (Bigelow) Beck var.
> > *floridana* (Wherry) Correll c

Florida ladies'-tresses

Texas east to Florida, north to North Carolina
Brown, P.M. 2001. *NANOJ* 7(1): 92–93.

known from only a single extant site in recent years

Spiranthes infernalis Sheviak

Ash Meadows ladies'-tresses

Nevada
Sheviak, C.J. 1989. *Rhodora* 91: 225–34.

federally threatened; endemic to a single area; overlooked?

Spiranthes lacera Rafinesque var. *lacera*

Neottia lacera Rafinesque

northern slender ladies'-tresses

Alberta east to Nova Scotia, south to Missouri and Virginia

leaves usually absent at flowering time

Spiranthes lacera Rafinesque var. *gracilis* (Bigelow) Luer

Ibidium beckii (Lindley) House
Ibidium gracile (Bigelow) House

Neottia gracilis Bigelow
Spiranthes beckii Lindley
Spiranthes gracilis (Bigelow) Beck c

southern slender ladies'-tresses

Kansas, Minnesota east to Maine and Nova Scotia, south to Texas and Georgia

Spiranthes laciniata (Small)
Ames

> *Gyrostachys laciniata* Small
> *Ibidium laciniatum* (Small)
House

lace-lipped ladies'-tresses

southern New Jersey south to
Florida, west to Texas

widespread and often common;
hairs ball-tipped

Spiranthes longilabris Lindley

> *Ibidium longilabre* (Lindley)
House

long-lipped ladies'-tresses

Virginia south to Florida, west to
Texas

widespread and scattered; flowers
intermittently

Spiranthes lucida (H.H. Eaton) Ames

Ibidium plantagineum (Rafinesque) House

Spiranthes plantaginea Rafinesque

shining ladies'-tresses

Wisconsin east to Nova Scotia, south to Kansas, Alabama, and West Virginia

bright yellow lip is diagnostic; calciphile

Spiranthes magnicamporum Sheviak

Great Plains ladies'-tresses

Manitoba east to southern Ontario, south to New Mexico, Texas, Pennsylvania, and Georgia

tall plants with very large flowers; leaves typically absent at flowering time

Spiranthes ochroleuca
(Rydberg) Rydberg

  Gyrostachys ochroleuca
Rydberg *ex* Britton
  Spiranthes cernua (Linnaeus)
L.C. Richard var. *ochroleuca*
(Rydberg) Ames c
  Spiranthes ×steigeri Correll

yellow ladies'-tresses

Michigan east to Nova Scotia,
south to Kentucky and South
Carolina

butterscotch underside of lip
helps to separate it from races
of *S. cernua*

Spiranthes odorata (Nuttall)
Lindley

  Spiranthes cernua (Linnaeus) L.C.
Richard var. *odorata* (Nuttall)
Correll c

fragrant ladies'-tresses

(New Jersey?) south to Florida, west
to Texas

often growing in standing water;
plants can be up to 1 meter in
height

Spiranthes ovalis Lindley var. *ovalis*

   Ibidium ovale (Lindley) House

southern oval ladies'-tresses

Arkansas south to Texas, east to
Florida

Catling, P.M. 1983. *Brittonia* 35:
   120–25.

very rare and local in the few states
in which it occurs; woodland habitat
unusual for *Spiranthes*

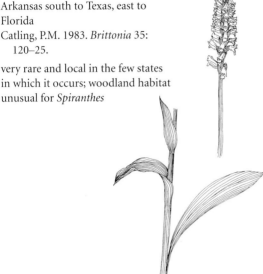

Spiranthes ovalis Lindley var.
erostellata Catling

northern oval ladies'-tresses

Wisconsin east to southern Ontario and
Maryland, south to Texas and northern
Florida

Catling, P.M. 1983. *Brittonia* 35: 120–25.

more widespread and often in second-
growth disturbed areas; usually in light
shade

Spiranthes parksii Correll

Navasota ladies'-tresses

Texas

Catling, P.M., and K.L.
McIntosh. 1979. *Sida*
8: 188–93.

federally listed as
endangered; rare
endemic to east-
central Texas

Spiranthes porrifolia Lindley

Spiranthes romanzoffiana
Chamisso var. *porrifolia* (Lindley)
Ames & Correll c

western ladies'-tresses

Washington south to California; east
to Idaho and Nevada

early summer flowering in open, hot,
seasonally dry areas

Spiranthes praecox (Walter) S. Watson

Ibidium praecox (Walter) House

giant ladies'-tresses

(New York, New Jersey?) south to Florida, west to southeastern Oklahoma and Texas

forma *albolabia* Brown & McCartney—white-lipped form Brown, P.M. 1995. *NANOJ* 1(1): 13.

typical flowers are snow-white with diverging green veins on the lip

Spiranthes romanzoffiana Chamisso

Gyrostachys stricta Rydberg

Ibidium strictum (Rydberg) House

Spiranthes stricta (Rydberg) A. Nelson *ex* J.M. Coulter & A. Nelson

hooded ladies'-tresses

Alaska east to Newfoundland; south to California, northern New Mexico, Indiana, Pennsylvania; Northern Ireland, Great Britain

widespread and often common throughout the northern states and provinces

Spiranthes sylvatica P.M. Brown

Spiranthes praecox (Walter) S. Watson misapplied

woodland ladies'-tresses

eastern Texas to Florida, north to southern Virginia

Brown, P.M. 2001. *NANOJ* 7(3): 193–205.

recently described; creamy green flowers have diverging green veins in the lip similar to *S. praecox;* habitat is shaded borders or deep woods

Spiranthes torta (Thunberg) Garay & Sweet

Ibidium tortile (Swartz) House

Spiranthes tortilis (Swartz) L.C. Richard c

southern ladies'-tresses

southern Florida; the Bahamas, West Indies, Central America

the only green-throated, summer-flowering *Spiranthes* in southern Florida

Spiranthes tuberosa Rafinesque

   Spiranthes grayi Ames c
   Spiranthes simplex A. Gray
   Spiranthes tuberosa var. *grayi* (Ames)
Fernald

little ladies'-tresses

Michigan east to Massachusetts, south to
Texas and Florida

purest white, crystalline flowers; leaves
absent at flowering time

Spiranthes vernalis Engelmann & Gray

   Ibidium vernale (Engelmann & Gray)
House

grass-leaved ladies'-tresses

Nebraska east to southern New Hampshire,
south to Texas and Florida; Mexico

widespread and in the southern states one of
the most common orchids; often in flower
somewhere within its range twelve months
of the year!

Hybrids:

Spiranthes ×*borealis* P.M. Brown
northern hybrid ladies'-tresses
(*S. casei* var. *casei* × *S. ochroleuca*)
Brown, P.M. 1995. *NANOJ* 1(4): 290.

Spiranthes ×*folsomii* P.M. Brown
Folsom's hybrid ladies'-tresses
(*S. longilabris* × *S. odorata*)
Brown, P.M. 2000. *NANOJ* 6(1): 16.

continued

Spiranthes ×intermedia Ames

intermediate hybrid ladies'-tresses

(*S. lacera* var. *gracilis* × *S. vernalis*)
Catling, P.M. 1978. *Rhodora* 80: 377–89.

Spiranthes ×itchetuckneensis P.M. Brown

Ichetucknee Springs hybrid ladies'-tresses

(*S. ovalis* var. *ovalis* × *S. odorata*)
Brown, P.M. 1999. *NANOJ* 5(4): 358–67.

Spiranthes ×meridionalis P.M. Brown

southern hybrid ladies'-tresses

(*S. vernalis* × *S. praecox*)
    Spiranthes ×australis P.M. Brown *nom. illeg.*
Brown, P.M. 1999. *NANOJ* 5(4): 358–67.
———. 2000. *NANOJ* 6(2): 139.

Spiranthes ×simpsonii Catling & Sheviak

Simpson's hybrid ladies'-tresses

(*S. lacera* var. *lacera* × *S. romanzoffiana*)
Catling, P.M., and C.J. Sheviak. 1993. *Lindleyana*
    8(2): 78–80.

Stenorrhynchos michuacanum (Llave & Lexarza) Lindley

   Dichromanthus michuacanus Salazar & Soto Arenas
   Spiranthes michuacana (Llave & Lexarza) Hemsley c, l, p, w

Michoacan ladies'-tresses

Arizona, Texas; Mexico

Coleman, R.A. 1996. *Orchids* 65(12): 1284–87.
Salazar, G.A., M.W. Chase, and M.A. Soto
    Arenas. 2002. *Lindleyana* 17(3): 173.

very local, but more frequent than
recently supposed

Tipularia discolor (Pursh) Nuttall

Tipularia unifolia Britton, Sterns, & Poggenberg

crane-fly orchis

Michigan east to Massachusetts, south to Texas and Florida

    forma *viridifolia* P.M. Brown— green-leaved form

Brown, P.M. 2000. *NANOJ* 6(4): 336–37.

asymmetrical flowers looking like dancing crane-flies; distinctive seer-sucker leaves absent at flowering time

Tolumnia bahamensis (Nash *ex* Britton & Millspaugh) G.J. Braem

    Oncidium bahamense Nash *ex* Britton & Millspaugh w

    Oncidium variegatum Swartz var. *bahamense* (Nash *ex* Britton & Millspaugh) Withner

    Oncidium variegatum Swartz misapplied c,l

    Tolumnia variegata (Swartz) Braem misapplied f

Florida's dancing lady

east-central Florida; the Bahamas

Ackerman, J. 2000. *Lindleyana* 15(2): 93.

Sauleda, R.P., and R.M. Adams. 1989. *Rhodora* 91(866): 188–200.

known only from a few sites on the Palm Beach/Martin County line, Florida

Trichocentrum carthagenense (Jacquin)
M.W. Chase & N.H. Williams

Lophiaris carthagenensis (Jacquin) G.A.
Braem

Oncidium carthagenense (Jacquin)
Swartz c, l, w

spread-eagle orchid

southern Florida; West Indies, Central
America, northern South America

Braem, G.J. 1993. *Schlechteriana* 4: 17.

Williams, N.H., M.W. Chase, T. Fulcher, and
    W.M. Whitten. 2001. *Lindleyana* 16(2):
    137.

a single collection by Small in 1916 near
Coot Bay, Monroe County, Florida; native?

Trichocentrum undulatum (Swartz)
Ackerman & M.W. Chase

> *Lophiaris maculata* (Aublet) Ackerman
> *Oncidium undulatum* (Swartz) Salisbury
> *Trichocentrum maculatum* (Aublet) M.W.

Chase & N.H. Williams *nom. illeg.*

> *Lophiaris lurida* (Lindley) G.J. Braem

misapplied

> *Oncidium luridum* Lindley misapplied c,

L, W

spotted mule-eared orchid

southern Florida; West Indies (Central
America, northern South America)

> forma *flavovirens* (P.M. Brown) P.M.
Brown—unspotted with a yellow-green
base

Ackerman, J. 2000. *Lindleyana* 15(2): 92–93.
Ackerman, J., and M.W. Chase. 2001.
> *Lindleyana* 16(4): 225.
Brown, P.M. 1995. *NANOJ* 1(2): 132.
———. 2000. *NANOJ* 6(4): 337.
———. 2001. *NANOJ* 7(3): 250.
———. 2001. *NANOJ* 7(4): 257.
Chase, M.W., and N.H. Williams. 2001.
> *Lindleyana* 16(3): 218.

this large, and often spectacular, plant has
recently undergone extensive nomenclatural
revisions

Triphora amazonica Schlechter

Triphora latifolia Luer *f.* L, W

wide-leaved noddingcaps

Florida; West Indies
Ackerman, J. 2000.
Lindleyana 15(2):
93–94.

the rarest of the diminutive *Triphora* species; currently known only in Florida from the original locality

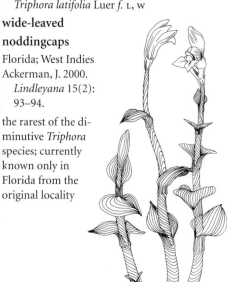

Triphora craigheadii Luer

Craighead's noddingcaps

Florida

a few scattered sites in central Florida

Triphora gentianoides (Swartz) Ames &
Schlechter

   Triphora cubensis (Reichenbach *f.*) Ames

least noddingcaps

southern Florida; West
Indies, Central America,
northern South America

spreading in southern and
central Florida, often in cul-
tivated areas; native?

Triphora rickettii Luer

   Triphora yucatanensis
Ames misapplied F

Rickett's noddingcaps

Florida

tiny yellow upright flowers
usually arranged in a cyme

Triphora trianthophora (Swartz) Rydberg subsp. *trianthophora*

Pogonia pendula (Mühlenberg *ex* Willdenow) Lindley
Triphora pendula (Mühlenberg *ex* Willdenow) Nuttall

three birds orchid

Iowa east to Maine, south to Texas and Florida
    forma *albidoflava* Keenan—white-flowered form
    forma *caerulea* P.M. Brown—blue-flowered form
    forma *rossii* P.M. Brown—multicolor form
Brown, P.M. 1999. *NANOJ* 5(1): 5.
———. 2001. *NANOJ* 7(1): 94–95.
Keenan, P. 1992. *Rhodora* 94: 38–39.
Medley, M.E. 1991. *Selbyana* 12: 102–3.

the most widespread of all *Triphora* species; usually flowers for a very brief time in midsummer, but in Florida colonies are in flower from late July until December

Tropidia polystachya (Swartz) Ames

many-flowered tropidia

southeastern Florida; West Indies, Mexico, Central America, northern South America

thought to be extirpated until a recent rediscovery south of Miami

Vanilla barbellata Reichenbach *f.*

Vanilla articulata Northrop

worm-vine, leafless vanilla

southern Florida; West Indies

leafless plants bear large showy flowers; usually in mangrove swamps

Vanilla dilloniana Correll

Vanilla eggersii Rolfe misapplied

Dillon's vanilla

southeastern Florida; West Indies

presumed extirpated; known only from cultivation

Vanilla mexicana Miller

Vanilla inodora Schiede ʟ, ᴡ

thin-leaved vanilla, scentless vanilla

southeastern Florida; West Indies, Central
America, northern South America

Heaton, J. 2001. *NANOJ* 7(3): 247–49.

currently known only from Martin
County, Florida; flowers unlike any other
Vanilla

Vanilla phaeantha Reichenbach f.

oblong-leaved vanilla

southwestern Florida; West Indies

found primarily in the Fakahatchee Swamp area in Florida; flowers
ephemeral and often closed by 10 A.M.

Vanilla planifolia Jackson *ex* Andrews*

Vanilla fragrans (Salisbury) Ames

commercial vanilla

southern Florida; West Indies, Central America, northern and western South America

persistent escape around Miami, Florida

Vanilla pompona Schiede*

southern vanilla

southeastern Florida; West Indies, Central America, northern and western South America

popular ornamental; occasional escape near Miami, Florida

Zeuxine strateumatica (Linnaeus) Schlechter*

lawn orchid

Texas east to Florida; Puerto Rico; southeastern Asia

the only annual in the Orchidaceae; most widespread
of all of the southern naturalized species; starts flowering in November and continues throughout the winter
and early spring

A Selection of Hybrids and Color, Leaf, and Growth Forms

1. *Amerorchis rotundifolia* forma *beckettiae*

2. *Amerorchis rotundifolia* forma *lineata*

3. *Arethusa bulbosa* forma *albiflora*

4. *Arethusa bulbosa* forma *subcaerulea*

5. *Bletia purpurea* forma *alba*

6. *Calypso bulbosa* var. *americana* forma *albiflora*

7. *Calypso bulbosa* var. *americana* forma *rosea*

8. *Cleistes divaricata* forma *leucantha*

9. *Corallorhiza maculata* var. *maculata* forma *flavida*

10. *Corallorhiza maculata* var. *occidentalis* forma *immaculata*

11. *Corallorhiza mertensiana* forma *albolabia*

12. *Corallorhiza striata* var. *striata* forma *eburnea*

13. *Corallorhiza wisteriana* forma *rubra*

14. *Cypripedium acaule*
forma *albiflorum*

15. *Cypripedium arietinum*
forma *biflorum*

16. *Cypripedium reginae*
forma *albolabium*

17. *Cypripedium* ×*alaskanum*

18. *Cypripedium* ×*andrewsii*

19. *Dactylorhiza aristata* var.
kodiakensis forma *perbracteata*

20. *Dactylorhiza majalis* subsp. *praetermissa* forma *albiflora*

21. *Encyclia tampensis* forma *albolabia*

22. *Epidendrum amphistomum*
forma *rubrifolium*

23. *Epipactis helleborine* forma *luteola*

24. *Galearis spectabilis*
forma *gordinierii*

25. *Galearis spectabilis*
forma *willeyi*

26. *Goodyera oblongifolia*
forma *reticulata*

27. *Listera australis* forma *scottii*

28. *Listera australis* forma *trifolia*

29. *Listera convallarioides* forma *trifolia*

30. *Listera cordata* var. *cordata*
forma *variegata*

31. *Listera* ×*veltmanii*

32. *Platanthera blephariglottis* var. *blephariglottis* forma *holopetala*

33. *Platanthera grandiflora* forma *albiflora*

34. *Platanthera hookeri* forma
abbreviata

35. *Platanthera ×andrewsii*

36. *Platanthera ×bicolor*

37. *Platanthera ×channellii*

38. *Platanthera* ×*keenanii*

39. *Pogonia ophioglossoides*
forma *albiflora*

40. *Pogonia ophioglossoides*
forma *brachypogon*

41. *Prosthechea cochleata*
var. *triandra* forma *albidoflava*

42. *Sacoila lanceolata* var. *lanceolata* forma *albidaviridis*

43. *Sacoila lanceolata* var. *lanceolata* forma *folsomii*

44. *Sacoila lanceolata* var. *paludicola* forma *aurea*

45. *Spiranthes praecox* forma *albolabia*

46. *Spiranthes ×borealis*

47. *Spiranthes ×folsomii*

48. *Spiranthes* ×*meridionalis*

49. *Triphora trianthophora* subsp. *trianthophora* forma *caerulea*

Using the Checklist as a Field Guide

For those who wish to use the checklist as a continental field guide the following keys are provided. The keys are intended to be used in the field rather than in the herbarium, and therefore many characters are utilized that directly relate to geography, habitat, and habit. The keys do not accommodate variants, that is, color forms, growth forms, or aberrant individuals. More details on most of the species can be found in any one of the many other books and journal articles listed in the bibliography. For those genera with more than one species or variety additional keys are provided after the generic key.

Choose your specimen carefully—neither the largest or smallest, nor the most unusual. The keys work best with an average plant. It may be necessary to consult some of these other works for additional drawings and photos to confirm an identification.

Difficulties may be encountered with some of the green-flowered *Platanthera* group, especially in the western states and provinces. These plants take a great deal of experience and still confound and confuse the best of us! The only *Spiranthes* that consistently poses a problem is *Spiranthes cernua* because of the morphological variation in different parts of its range.

Presenting keys to all of the species in North America has been somewhat problematic in that there are several other excellent keys available in the current literature. Sometimes a spade-shaped lip is simply a spade-shaped lip, and although I have endeavored not to quote directly from the keys of other authors, avoiding direct quotes has become difficult in a few instances. The key to the three varieties of *Cypripedium parviflorum* is based on that of Charles J. Sheviak, with permission.

Key to the Wild Orchids

* indicates genera that are non-native

Plants Epiphytic

1a	plants epiphytic . . . 2
1b	plants terrestrial . . . 20

2a	plants vining or climbing (roots may be in ground but the majority of the plant is epiphytic) . . . *Vanilla,* key 31
2b	plants not vining or climbing . . . 3

3a	plants without pseudobulbs . . . 4
3b	plants with pseudobulbs . . . 9

4a	plants leafless . . . 5
4b	plants with leaves . . . 7

5a	flowers white, large and showy . . . *Dendrophylax*
5b	flowers otherwise, small . . . 6

6a	flowers peachy orange, several crowded into spikes . . . *Campylocentrum*
6b	flowers translucent yellow, in small clusters . . . *Harrisella*

7a	flowers very small, arranged in spikes . . . 8
7b	flowers variously arranged, often in terminal clusters or spikes . . . *Epidendrum,* key 12

8a	flowers white, leaves large . . . *Pleurothallis*
8b	flowers crimson, leaves small . . . *Lepanthopsis*

9a	inflorescence terminal from the tip of the pseudobulb . . . 10
9b	inflorescence axillary from the base of the pseudobulb . . . 13

10a   flowers small, yellow, arranged in branched one-sided racemes . . . *Polystachya*

10b   flowers otherwise, variously arranged . . . 11

11a   lip uppermost or flowers barred with brown . . . *Prosthechea*, key 26

11b   lip lowermost and flowers not barred with brown . . . 12

12a   pseudobulbs flattened and wrinkled . . . *Laelia*

12b   pseudobulbs rounded . . . *Encyclia*, key 11

13a   inflorescence pendent . . . 14

13b   inflorescence in sessile clusters, erect or arching . . . 15

14a   flowers small, less than 1 cm, brown, in a pendent spike . . . *Bulbophyllum*

14b   flowers larger, more than 1 cm, in a pendent or arching raceme . . . *Macradenia*

15a   leaves slender, inrolled, and sharp-tipped; pseudobulbs minute and hidden within the leaf bases . . . 16

15b   leaves and/or pseudobulbs otherwise . . . 17

16a   plant scandent, lip proportionate to petals and sepals . . . *Tolumnia*

16b   plant a twig epiphyte, lip much larger than petals or sepals . . . *Ionopsis*

17a   flowers small in few- to many-flowered sessile clusters at the bases of the leaves . . . *Maxillaria*, key 21

17b   flowers otherwise . . . 18

18a   leaves erect, stiff, coriaceous, persisting . . . *Trichocentrum*, key 29

18b   leaves otherwise . . . 19

19a   leaves plicate, annual, new growth emerging at flowering time; flowers in a branched panicle . . . *Cyrtopodium*, key 9

19b   leaves persistent; flowers on an unbranched arching raceme . . . *Brassia*

Plants Terrestrial

20a   lip inflated or sac shaped . . . 21

20b   lip otherwise . . . 24

21a	flowers small, whitish, and in spikes . . . *Goodyera,* key 14
21b	flowers otherwise . . . 22

22a	lip a distinct slipper . . . *Cypripedium,* key 8
22b	lip spade-shaped or boat-shaped . . . 23

23a	lip spade-shaped, leaves multiple . . . *Epipactis,* key 13
23b	lip boat-shaped, leaf solitary . . . *Calypso,* key 3

Leaves Lacking at Flowering Time

24a	(green) leaves (apparently) lacking at flowering time; stem bracts may be present . . . 25
24b	(green) leaves present at flowering time . . . 41

25a	plants lacking chlorophyll . . . 26
25b	plants with chlorophyll . . . 28

26a	entire plant white (including leaves), lip with a yellow blotch . . . *Cephalanthera*
26b	plants various colors, leafless . . . 27

27a	flower with a mentum . . . *Corallorhiza,* key 6
27b	flower lacking a mentum . . . *Hexalectris,* key 16

28a	spur or mentum present . . . 29
28b	spur or mentum lacking . . . 32

29a	flowers asymmetrical . . . *Tipularia*
29b	flowers symmetrical . . . 30

30a	flower small, less than 1 cm, in open to dense spikes . . . *Piperia,* key 22
30b	flowers larger, 1+ cm . . . 31

31a	flowers tubular, mentum short . . . *Sacoila,* key 27
31b	flowers not tubular, mentum/spur fat and rounded . . . *Galeandra*

32a	flowers few (usually less than 10), terminal, loosely arranged in an open raceme . . . 33
32b	flowers numerous (usually 10+ to 60), arranged in a spike, often dense and/or spiraled . . . 37

33a   flowers large (over 1 cm), usually solitary (rarely 2–4) . . . *Arethusa*
33b   flowers otherwise . . . 34

34a   flowers cleistogamous . . . *Basiphyllaea*
34b   flowers chasmogamous . . . 35

35a   flowers non-resupinate, held horizontal to the axis . . . *Ponthieva,* key 25
35b   flowers otherwise . . . 36

36a   flowers small and translucent white with a prominent red spot on the underside of the lip . . . *Schiedeella*
36b   flowers otherwise . . . 37

37a   inflorescence a spike, often with many (20–60) small flowers . . . 38
37b   inflorescence a raceme with fewer flowers (10+/-) . . . 40

38a   inflorescence of small, tubular, white or cream flowers with fringed lips, usually in a loose to dense spiral . . . *Spiranthes,* key 28
38b   inflorescence otherwise . . . 39

39a   petals and sepal undulate . . . *Deiregyne*
39b   petals and sepals not undulate . . . *Stenorrhynchos*

40a   rachis glabrous; leaves withering or withered at flowering time . . . *Aplectrum*
40b   rachis pubescent . . . *Ponthieva,* key 25

Leaves Present at Flowering Time

Spur or Mentum Present

41a   spur or mentum present . . . 42
41b   spur or mentum lacking . . . 56

42a   inflorescence terminal on a leafy stem . . . 43
42b   inflorescence terminal on a scape (leafless stem) . . . 49

43a   lip entire, divided, or fringed, but NEVER notched or toothed, nor ever forming colonies of basal rosettes . . . *Platanthera,* key 23
43b   plants otherwise . . . 44

44a   lip oblong and notched at tip . . . *Coeloglossum,* key 5

44b   lip otherwise . . . 45

45a   lip 3–toothed, flowers small and nodding on a crowded spike . . . *Pseudorchis*

45b   lip otherwise . . . 46

46a   petals deeply cleft or toothed, sterile plants forming distinctive colonies of large basal rosettes (southeastern United States) . . . *Habenaria,* key 15

46b   plants otherwise . . . 47

47a   flowers white in short spikes, with a thick bulbous spur . . . *Platythelys,* key 24

47b   flowers otherwise . . . 48

48a   flowers pink, spotted with deeper pink (Connecticut waif) . . . *Gymnadenia**

48b   flowers otherwise . . . *Platanthera,* key 23

49a   leaves with distinct long petioles . . . 50

49b   leaves otherwise . . . 51

50a   lip margin with a delicate, short fringe . . . *Eltroplectris*

50b   lip margin entire . . . *Pelexia*

51a   leaf solitary . . . 52

51b   leaves multiple . . . 54

52a   leaf with prominent white markings . . . *Oeceoclades**

52b   leaf unmarked . . . 53

53a   flowers green . . . *Platanthera,* key 23

53b   flowers white or pink . . . *Amerorchis*

54a   leaves basal with the scape arising from the center of the leaves . . . 55

54b   scape arises apart from the leaves; flowers with a prominent crest on the lip . . . *Eulophia*

55a   flowers brick red to scarlet . . . *Sacoila,* key 27

55b   flowers pink, purple, and/or white . . . *Galearis*

Spur or Mentum Lacking

56a	pseudobulbs present, although they may be well hidden in the leaf bases . . . 57
56b	pseudobulbs lacking . . . 60

57a	leaves long, slender, and grass-like . . . *Oncidium*
57b	leaves otherwise . . . 58

58a	lip inrolled to form a tube . . . *Phaius**
58b	lip otherwise . . . 59

59a	inflorescence a slender spike or flowers orange and green . . . *Malaxis,* key 20
59b	inflorescence a spike or raceme of purple flowers . . . *Liparis,* key 18

60a	leaves two . . . 61
60b	leaves three or more . . . 62

61a	petals filiform, thread-like . . . *Liparis,* key 18
61b	petals various configurations, but not filiform . . . *Platanthera,* key 23

Leaves Basal

62a	leaves essentially basal or extending up the lower 1/4 of the stem and rapidly reduced to leafy bracts . . . 63
62b	leaves essentially cauline . . . 71

63a	leaves forming a distinctive basal rosette . . . 64
63b	leaves otherwise . . . 65

64a	leaves few, flowers white or cream in spikes, often spiraled . . . *Spiranthes,* key 28
64b	leaves numerous, flowers pink to purple . . . *Spathoglottis**

65a	flowers non-resupinate . . . *Cranichis*
65b	flowers resupinate . . . 66

66a	flowers brilliant carmine-red . . . *Dichromanthus*
66b	flowers otherwise . . . 67

67a   flowers flat, held perpendicular to the axis on distinctive petioles . . . *Ponthieva*, key 25

67b   flowers otherwise . . . 68

68a   flowers white with a rounded ball-like appearance . . . *Prescottia*

68b   flowers otherwise . . . 69

69a   flowers white with distinctive green median stripes . . . *Beloglottis*

69b   flowers otherwise . . . 70

70a   flowers copper-colored, lip concave . . . *Mesadenus*

70b   flowers white to green to brown, lip flat . . . *Cyclopogon*, key 7

Leaves Cauline

71a   flowers non-resupinate . . . *Calopogon*, key 2

71b   flowers resupinate . . . 72

72a   leaves opposite or whorled . . . 73

72b   leaves solitary or alternate . . . 74

73a   leaves 2, opposite . . . *Listera*, key 19

73b   leaves 5–7, whorled . . . *Isotria*, key 17

74a   leaves solitary, bracts may be present . . . 75

74b   leaves multiple . . . 77

75a   inflorescence a spike raceme or corymb of very small flowers . . . *Malaxis*, key 20

75b   inflorescence otherwise . . . 76

76a   lip projecting forward with the side inrolled to form a tube . . . *Cleistes*, key 4

76b   lip with a distinctive fringed beard . . . *Pogonia*

77a   inflorescence terminating a leafy stem; in a raceme, spike or cluster rarely individual . . . 80

77b   inflorescence an axillary scape . . . 78

78a   flowers greenish yellow and purplish black on tall scapes . . . *Pteroglossaspis*

78b   flowers otherwise, usually shades of pink and purple . . . 79

79a   lip with distinctive keels or ridges . . . *Bletia,* key 1
79b   lip with a distinct isthmus . . . *Spathoglottis**

80a   leaves plicate, lip striate, flowers purple . . . *Bletilla**
80b   otherwise . . . 81

81a   leaves small, oval, or scale-like . . . *Triphora,* key 30
81b   leaves otherwise . . . 82

82a   leaves clustered along an apparently semi-woody stem, flowers in panicles
       . . . *Tropidia*
82b   leaves arranged otherwise . . . 83

83a   flowers white with yellow on the lip . . . *Zeuxine**
83b   plants otherwise . . . 84

84a   flowers white . . . *Govenia*
84b   flowers purple, rarely white . . . *Dactylorhiza,* key 10

Keys to those genera having more than one species, subspecies, or variety

Key 1

Bletia

1a   lip clearly longer than the undulate petals . . . **slender pine-pink,** *B. patula*
1b   lip equal to or shorter than the non-undulate petals . . . 2

2a   lip with 5 yellow crests, only the 3 central ones extending onto the midlobe
      . . . **Haitian pine-pink,** *B. florida*
2b   lip with 5–7 yellow crests, all extending onto the midlobe . . . **pine-pink,** *B.
      purpurea*

Key 2

Calopogon

1a   the vast majority of the flowers open simultaneously . . . 2
1b   1–4 flowers open at a time, plants flowering over several weeks . . . 3

2a   petals widest below the middle . . . 4

2b   petals widest above the middle . . . **many-flowered grass-pink,** *C. multiflorus*

3a   floral bracts 2–4 mm, plants of the southeastern coastal plain . . . **bearded grass-pink,** *C. barbatus*

3b   floral bracts 4–8 mm, plants primarily of the Midwest . . . **Oklahoma grass-pink,** *C. oklahomensis*

4a   petals narrow and strongly ascending . . . **pale grass-pink,** *C. pallidus*

4b   petals broad and spreading . . . 5

5a   leaves flat, about 1 cm wide; apex of lip not whitened (except in forma *albiflorus*) . . . **common grass-pink,** *C. tuberosus* var. *tuberosus*

5b   leaves very narrow (actually inrolled), appearing about 2–3 mm wide; apex of lip whitened; plants of southern Florida marls and pinelands . . . **Simpson's grass-pink,** *C. tuberosus* var. *simpsonii*

Key 3

Calypso

1a   beard yellow . . . **eastern fairy-slipper,** *C. bulbosa* var. *americana*

1b   beard white . . . **western fairy-slipper,** *C. bulbosa* var. *occidentalis*

Key 4

Cleistes

1a   column 13–19 mm long; lip 26 mm long; leaf and bract broadly lanceolate . . . **upland spreading pogonia,** *C. bifaria*

1b   column 21–25 mm long; lip 34–56 mm long; leaf and bract narrowly lanceolate . . . **spreading pogonia,** *C. divaricata*

Key 5

Coeloglossum

1a   lower floral bracts equal to flower or slightly longer; northern . . . **northern bracted green orchis,** *C. viride* var. *viride*

1b   lower floral bracts greatly exceeding flowers; widespread . . . **long bracted green orchis,** *C. viride* var. *virescens*

Key 6

Corallorhiza

1a   flowers cleistogamous . . . 2
1b   flowers chasmogamous . . . 3

2a   flower very small, less than 3 mm, autumn flowering . . . **autumn coralroot**, *C. odontorhiza* var. *odontorhiza*
2b   flowers 5–10 mm, summer flowering, western Virginia and eastern West Virginia . . . **Bentley's coralroot**, *C. bentleyi*

3a   lip solid color (not white) or striped . . . 4
3b   lip otherwise . . . 6

4a   lip striped . . . 5
4b   lip solid purple, lavender, or pink . . . **western coralroot**, *C. mertensiana*

5a   flowers red to scarlet; open fully . . . **striped coralroot**, *C. striata* var. *striata*
5b   flowers dusky tan and dull red; not wide spreading . . . **Vreeland's striped coralroot**, *C. striata* var. *vreelandii*

6a   lip usually unspotted, spring flowering . . . **early coralroot**, *C. trifida*
6b   lip spotted . . . 7

7a   winter and spring flowering . . . **Wister's coralroot**, *C. wisteriana*
7b   summer and autumn flowering . . . 8

8a   petals and sepals distinct, late spring–summer flowering . . . 9
8b   petals and sepals indistinct, autumn flowering . . . 11

9a   lip with parallel sides, mid–late summer . . . **spotted coralroot**, *C. maculata* var. *maculata*
9b   lip broadened towards apex, late spring–early summer . . . 10

10a   lip spotted randomly throughout the expanded mid-lobe; mentum 1.5–2.5 mm long; plants widespread . . . **western spotted coralroot**, *C. maculata* var. *occidentalis*
10b   lip spotted primarily on the margin of the expanded mid-lobe; mentum 2.0–3.5 mm long; plants of southeastern Arizona . . . **Mexican spotted coralroot** . . . *C. maculata* var. *mexicana*

11a   lip prominent, flowers chasmogamous . . . **Pringle's autumn coralroot,** *C. odontorhiza* var. *pringlei*

11b   lip not prominent, often undeveloped . . . **autumn coralroot,** *C. odontorhiza* var. *odontorhiza*

Key 7

Cyclopogon

1a   petals and sepals divergent . . . **speckled ladies'-tresses,** *C. cranichoides*

1b   petals and sepals appressed . . . **tall neottia,** *C. elatus*

Key 8

Cypripedium

1a   leaves basal . . . **pink lady's-slipper,** *C. acaule*

1b   leaves cauline . . . 2

2a   leaves usually 2 (rarely 3) . . . 3

2b   leaves 3 or more . . . 5

3a   flowers solitary . . . 4

3b   flowers in clusters . . . **clustered lady's-slipper,** *C. fasciculatum*

4a   lip white with cranberry markings . . . **spotted lady's-slipper,** *C. guttatum*

4b   lip cream with brown markings . . . **yellow spotted lady's-slipper,** *C. yatabeanum*

5a   sepals and petals white, lip shades of pink . . . **showy lady's-slipper,** *C. reginae*

5b   sepals and petals otherwise . . . 6

6a   lip white, often with markings of purple or crimson . . . 7

6b   lip yellow . . . 12

7a   petals marked with purple . . . 8

7b   petals unmarked . . . 10

8a   lip streaked with lavender . . . **small white lady's-slipper,** *C. candidum*

8b   lip unstreaked (may be spotted) . . . 9

9a   flowers large, lip 4.1–6.5 cm . . . **ivory-lipped lady's-slipper,** *C. kentuckiense*

9b   flowers moderate in size; lip 1.5–4.0 cm . . . **mountain lady's-slipper,** *C. montanum*

10a   lip veined and spotted with purple, sepals 3 . . . **ram's-head lady's-slipper,** *C. arietinum*

10b   lip unmarked . . . 11

11a   flowers few, usually 1 or 2 (3) . . . **sparrow's egg lady's-slipper,** *C. passerinum*

11b   flowers numerous, (3)6–18(22) . . . **California lady's-slipper,** *C. californicum*

12a   flowers very large, lip orbicular . . . **ivory-lipped lady's-slipper,** *C. kentuckiense*

12b   flowers otherwise, lip oval to oblong . . . 13

13a   outer surface of sheathing bract densely silvery-pubescent when young; sepals and petals variously marked; scent moderate to faint, rose or musty . . . 14

13b   outer surface of sheathing bract sparsely pubescent to glabrous when young, flowers small, lip 15–29 mm long; sepals and petals usually suffused with dark reddish brown or madder; scent intensely sweet; plants of calcareous fens and other mesic to limy wetlands; western and northern New England to the northern Cordillera northward . . . **northern small yellow lady's-slipper,** *C. parviflorum* var. *makasin*

14a   flowers commonly large, lip to 54 mm long, but very small in some northern plants; sepals and petals unmarked to spotted, striped or reticulately marked with reddish brown or madder; plants of a variety of habitats, usually mesic to calcareous, woodlands or open sites in limestone or gypsum; through the range of the species . . . **large yellow lady's-slipper,** *C. parviflorum* var. *pubescens*

14b   flowers small, lip 22–34 mm long; sepals and petals usually densely spotted with dark reddish brown appearing uniformly dark; plants of dry deciduous more acidic sites than var. *pubescens;* southern New England to Kansas southward . . . **southern small yellow lady's-slipper,** *C. parviflorum* var. *parviflorum*

Key 9

Cyrtopodium

1a   flowers pure yellow . . . **yellow cowhorn orchid**, *C. polyphyllum*
1b   flowers heavily spotted . . . **cowhorn orchid**, *C. punctatum*

Key 10

Dactylorhiza

1a   plants of Alaska . . . 2
1b   plants of Ontario and Newfoundland . . . 3

2a   lip spotted with a prominent emarginate tip, leaves usually unspotted; primarily on the mainland . . . **Fischer's orchid**, *D. aristata* var. *aristata*
2b   lip unspotted, broadly tapers to tip, leaves heavily spotted; primarily on Kodiak Island . . . **Kodiak orchid**, *D. aristata* var. *kodiakensis*

3a   leaves unmarked or moderately spotted; plants of Tilt Cove, Newfoundland . . . **southern marsh orchid**, *D. majalis* subsp. *praetermissa*
3b   leaves heavily spotted; plants of Timmins, Ontario, and St. John's, Newfoundland . . . **leopard marsh orchid**, *D. majalis* var. *junialis*

Key 11

Encyclia

1a   flowers dingy yellow–reddish-brown; lip entire, oblong . . . **rufous butterfly orchid**, *E. rufa*
1b   flowers yellow, white, and brown; lip 3-lobed, fan-shaped, and striped with purple . . . **Florida butterfly orchid**, *E. tampensis*

Key 12

Epidendrum

1a   inflorescence a many-flowered umbel . . . 2
1b   inflorescence otherwise . . . 4

2a   lip fringed or lacerated . . . **climbing epidendrum**, *E.* cf. *radicans*
2b   lip entire, although often lobed . . . 3

3a inflorescence long-stemmed; flowers bronzy-green . . . **dingy-flowered star orchid,** *E. amphistomum*

3b inflorescence short-stemmed; flowers watery-green . . . **Florida star orchid,** *E. floridense*

4a inflorescence a few-flowered cluster or flowers individual . . . 5

4b inflorescence a spike . . . 7

5a flowers large and showy with a strongly lobed, white lip . . . **night-fragrant epidendrum,** *E. nocturnum*

5b flowers otherwise . . . 6

6a flowers several in small, crowded, cone-like clusters . . . **cone-bearing epidendrum,** *E. strobiliferum*

6b flower individual at tips of long, trailing branches . . . **Acuña's star orchid,** *E. acunae*

7a spike a tight, zigzag arrangement . . . **rigid epidendrum,** *E. rigidum*

7b spike loose and open in arrangement . . . 8

8a flower watery green to greenish yellow, day fragrant . . . **green-fly orchis,** *E. magnoliae* var. *magnoliae*

8b flowers highly colored with bronze and pink, night fragrant . . . **bronze green-fly orchis,** *E. magnoliae* var. *mexicanum*

Key 13

Epipactis

1a lip 3-lobed . . . **stream orchid,** *E. gigantea*

1b lip not 3-lobed . . . 2

2a distal segment of the lip saccate, the sides rolled inward . . . **broad-leaved helleborine,** *E. helleborine*

2b distal segment of the lip spade-shaped . . . **red helleborine,** *E. atrorubens*

Key 14

Goodyera

1a flowers in a dense spike . . . 2

1b flowers in a lax spike . . . 3

2a   spike 1-sided . . . **giant rattlesnake orchis**, *G. oblongifolia*
2b   spike otherwise . . . **downy rattlesnake orchis**, *G. pubescens*

3a   spike 1-sided . . . **lesser rattlesnake orchis**, *G. repens*
3b   spike spiraled . . . **checkered rattlesnake orchis**, *G. tesselata*

Key 15

Habenaria

1a   lip and/or petals divided into linear, threadlike segments . . . 2
1b   lip and/or petals merely toothed . . . **toothed habenaria**, *H. odontopetala*

2a   leaves essentially basal or rapidly reduced upward; spur swollen . . . **false water-spider orchid**, *H. distans*
2b   leaves extending up the stem and gradually reduced in size; spur not swollen . . . 3

3a   spur equal to the ovary; plants of wet habitats . . . **water spider orchid**, *H. repens*
3b   spur distinctly longer than the ovary . . . 4

4a   anterior division of the lateral petal less than twice (10–18 mm) the length of the posterior division (6–9 mm); spur typically less than 10 cm (in living material); plants of open pinelands, hedgerows, and fields . . . **Michaux's orchid**, *H. quinqueseta*
4b   anterior division of the lateral petal more than twice (20–24 mm) the length of the posterior division (8–11 mm); flowers, when viewed straight on, with a distinct rectangular aspect; spur often greater than 10 cm (in living material); plants of rich mesic hardwood hammocks . . . **long-horned habenaria**, *H. macroceratitis*

Key 16

Hexalectris

1a   petals greater than 12 mm . . . 2
1b   petals less than 12 mm . . . **shining crested coralroot**, *H. nitida*

2a   lip with yellow longitudinal crests . . . **Texas purple-spike**, *H. warnockii*
2b   lip with white or purple longitudinal crests . . . 3

3a lip deeply 3-lobed . . . 5
3b lip shallowly 3-lobed and/or flowers cleistogamous . . . 4

4a flowers fully open; plants widespread throughout the southern United
   States . . . **crested coralroot,** *H. spicata* var. *spicata*
4b flowers cleistogamous or rarely partially open; plants of southern Arizona
   and Texas . . . **Arizona crested coralroot,** *H. spicata* var. *arizonica*

5a petals and sepals pink to purple . . . **Greenman's crested coralroot,** *H. gran-*
   diflora
5b petals and sepals otherwise . . . **recurved crested coralroot,** *H. revoluta*

Key 17

Isotria

1a sepals greenish-yellow; one and one-half times as long as the petals or
   shorter . . . **small whorled pogonia,** *I. medeoloides*
1b sepals purple; two or more times as long as the petals . . . **large whorled
   pogonia,** *I. verticillata*

Key 18

Liparis

1a flowers chocolate/purple; plants of rich woodlands and swamps . . . 2
1b flowers yellow/green; plants of moist areas . . . **Löesel's twayblade,** *L.*
   loeselii

2a flowers in a slender spike; plants of Florida . . . **tall twayblade,** *L. elata*
2b flowers in a loose raceme; plants of rich eastern woodlands . . . **lily-leaved
   twayblade,** *L. liliifolia*

Key 19

Listera

1a lip deeply cleft to more than half its length . . . 2
1b lip shallowly cleft to less than half its length . . . 3

2a lip about twice as long as petals . . . **heart-leaved twayblade,** *L. cordata*
2b lip about four times as long as petals . . . **southern twayblade,** *L. australis*

3a   lip with parallel sides, auricled at base . . . 4

3b   lip tapered from summit to base, not auricled at base . . . 5

4a   lip with a prominent darker green median stripe . . . **northern twayblade,** *L. borealis*

4b   lip entirely green with prominent auricles . . . **auricled twayblade,** *L. auriculata*

5a   lip bend downward . . . **common twayblade,** *L. ovata*

5b   lip thrust forward . . . 6

6a   lip entire or barely emarginate . . . **northwestern twayblade,** *L. caurina*

6b   lip distinctly cleft or notched . . . 7

7a   leaves rounded, usually longer than the peduncle of the raceme; plants of northern cool mossy woods and streamsides . . . **broad-lipped twayblade,** *L. convallarioides*

7b   leaves kidney-shaped, much shorter than the peduncle of the raceme; plants of northern New Jersey and Pennsylvania southward in wet woods or thickets . . . **Small's twayblade,** *L. smallii*

Key 20

Malaxis

1a   inflorescence a slender spike . . . 2

1b   inflorescence otherwise . . . 8

2a   flowers reddish purple . . . 3

2b   flowers otherwise . . . 4

3a   flowers not papillose, lip broadly acuminate, auricles narrow pointing up; plants of the mountains of Arizona and New Mexico . . . **purple adder's-mouth,** *M. porphyrea*

3b   flowers papillose, lip narrowly acuminate, auricles broad held to side; plants of the Chisos Mountains of Texas . . . **Wendt's adder's-mouth,** *M. wendtii*

4a   leaves two . . . 5

4b   leaf solitary . . . 7

5a   plants of cold northern bogs, woods, and meadows . . . 6

5b   plants of wet woodlands and forested floodplains; southeastern United States . . . **Florida adder's-mouth,** *M. spicata*

6a   plants greater than 5 cm . . . **two-leaved adder's-mouth,** *M. diphyllos*

6b   plants less than 5 cm . . . **bog adder's-mouth,** *M. paludosa*

7a   plants of montane woodlands in the southwestern United States (and Mexico) . . . **rat-tailed adder's-mouth,** *M. soulei*

7b   plants of wetter areas; circumboreal . . . **white adder's-mouth,** *M. brachypoda*

8a   plants of the eastern United States and Canada . . . 9

8b   plants of the southwestern United States (and Mexico) . . . 10

9a   inflorescence an elongated cluster or raceme; lower flowers persisting after anthesis . . . **Bayard's adder's-mouth,** *M. bayardii*

9b   inflorescence a flat-topped cluster; lower flowers withering after anthesis . . . **green adder's-mouth,** *M. unifolia*

10a   inflorescence a flat-topped cluster . . . **clustered adder's-mouth,** *M. corymbosa*

10b   inflorescence an open raceme . . . **fir-dwelling adder's-mouth,** *M. abieticola*

Key 21

Maxillaria

1a   leaves arranged in a loose fan, flowers individual from base of the leaves, flowers often cleistogamous . . . **false butterfly orchid,** *M. crassifolia*

1b   leaves arranged along a creeping stem, flowers clustered . . . **densely-flowered maxillaria,** *M. parviflora*

Key 22

Piperia

1a   spur distinctly exceeding lip . . . 2

1b   spur equal to or shorter than lip . . . 5

2a   sepals white with green central stripe . . . 3

2b   sepals green, yellow-green, or translucent . . . 4

3a   spur held horizontal to scape . . . **flat-spurred piperia**, *P. transversa*

3b   spur decurrent along stem . . . **elegant piperia**, *P. elegans* subsp. *elegans*

4a   petals and dorsal sepal overlapping about 2/3 . . . **Michael's piperia**, *P. michaelii*

4b   petals and dorsal sepal overlapping about 1/3 . . . **long-spurred piperia**, *P. elongata*

5a   sepals white with green central stripe . . . 6

5b   sepals green, yellow-green, or translucent . . . 8

6a   raceme laxly flowered, often secund or nearly so . . . **slender white piperia**, *P. candida*

6b   raceme cylindrical; plants of central California coast . . . 7

7a   petals straight and spreading; endemic in northern Monterey County . . . **Yadon's piperia**, *P. yadonii*

7b   petals falcate and incurved; endemic to Point Reyes, Marin County . . . **Point Reyes piperia**, *P. elegans* subsp. *decurtata*

8a   petals nearly linear . . . **lace orchid**, *P. leptopetala*

8b   petals otherwise . . . 9

9a   lip broadly spatulate and flat; plants of southern California chaparral . . . **Cooper's stout-spire orchid**, *P. cooperi*

9b   lip upcurved at tip . . . 10

10a   spur very short, 1–2 mm; endemic to California . . . **Coleman's piperia**, *P. colemanii*

10b   spur +/- equaling lip, 2–4 mm; widespread . . . **Alaskan piperia**, *P. unalascensis*

Key 23

Platanthera

Note: Students of the *Platanthera hyperborea-dilatata* complex, that is, *P. hyperborea, aquilonis, dilatata, huronensis, stricta,* and *sparsiflora,* should carefully consult Sheviak's work in *FNA;* this key considers typical specimens, but cannot always work with all of the variation caused by local gene flow.

1a	lip margin entire . . . 15
1b	lip margin variously fringed, eroded, lacerate, or toothed . . . 2

2a	lip 3-lobed . . . 10
2b	lip unlobed, the margin variously fringed, eroded, lacerate, or toothed . . . 3

3a	lip conspicuously fringed . . . 4
3b	lip erose or lacerated but not fringed . . . 9

4a	flowers white . . . 5
4b	flowers yellow or orange . . . 6

5a	lip with a very short isthmus; fringe lacerate; spur usually less than 26 mm; widespread in northeastern United States and Canada . . . **northern white fringed orchis**, *P. blephariglottis* var. *blephariglottis*
5b	lip narrowed to an extended isthmus; fringe delicately filiform; spur usually exceeding 30 mm; southeastern coastal plain . . . **southern white fringed orchis**, *P. blephariglottis* var. *conspicua*

6a	spur greatly exceeding the lip . . . **orange fringed orchis**, *P. ciliaris*
6b	spur equal to or less than the lip . . . 7

7a	flowers pale yellow to ivory . . . **pale fringed orchis**, *P. pallida*
7b	flowers brilliant yellow or orange . . . 8

8a	spur 8–17 mm long; spur orifice circular . . . **orange crested orchis**, *P. cristata*
8b	spur 4–10 mm; spur orifice keyhole-shaped . . . **Chapman's fringed orchis**, *P. chapmanii*

9a	flowers white . . . **monkey-face orchis**, *P. integrilabia*
9b	flowers yellow . . . **yellow fringeless orchis**, *P. integra*

10a	petals entire, lip deeply lacerate; flowers greenish white to cream green . . . **green fringed orchis**, *P. lacera*
10b	petals shallowly fringed at the apex . . . 11

11a	lip merely erose . . . **purple fringeless orchis**, *P. peramoena*
11b	lip distinctly fringed or lacerate . . . 12

12a   flowers typical shades of purple . . . 13
12b   flowers white . . . 14

13a   lip margin fringed less than 1/3 the length; spur orifice circular . . . **large purple fringed orchis**, *P. grandiflora*
13b   lip margin fringed more than 1/3 the length; spur orifice a transverse dumbbell . . . **small purple fringed orchis**, *P. psycodes*

14a   petals white, sepals green to whitish green, petals obovate; spur to 22 mm; plants primarily east of the Mississippi River . . . **eastern prairie fringed orchis**, *P. leucophaea*
14b   petals and sepals creamy white, petals flabellate; spur to 55 mm; plants primarily west of the Mississippi River . . . **western prairie fringed orchis**, *P. praeclara*

15a   lip with a distinct tubercle . . . 16
15b   lip otherwise . . . 17

16a   floral bracts usually equal to or shorter than the flowers . . . **southern tubercled orchis**, *P. flava* var. *flava*
16b   floral bracts longer than the flowers . . . **northern tubercled orchis**, *P. flava* var. *herbiola*

17a   lip emarginate or shallowly 3-lobed . . . 18
17b   lip otherwise . . . 19

18a   leaves multiple; inflorescence lax . . . **little club-spur orchis**, *P. clavellata* var. *clavellata*
18b   leaf solitary; inflorescence dense . . . **northern club-spur orchis**, *P. clavellata* var. *ophioglossoides*

19a   flowers non-resupinate (lip uppermost) . . . **snowy orchis**, *P. nivea*
19b   flowers resupinate (lip lowermost) . . . 20

20a   leaves basal . . . 21
20b   leaves cauline . . . 27

21a   leaf solitary . . . 22
21b   leaves 2 or more . . . 23

22a   lip slender, lanceolate . . . **blunt-leaved rein orchis**, *P. obtusata* subsp. *obtusata*

22b   lip broader, rhombic-lanceolate; plants of northern Alaska . . . **few-flowered blunt-leaved rein orchis**, *P. obtusata* subsp. *oligantha*

23a   flowers small, less than 1 cm . . . 24
23b   flowers larger, greater than 1 cm . . . 25

24a   spur stout . . . **Chamisso's orchid**, *P. chorisiana*
24b   spur slender . . . **Behring orchid**, *P. tipuloides* var. *behringiana*

25a   lip triangular . . . **Hooker's orchis**, *P. hookeri*
25b   lip oblong . . . 26

26a   spur less than 28 mm long . . . **pad-leaved orchis**, *P. orbiculata*
26b   spur greater than 28 mm long . . . **Goldie's pad-leaved orchis**, *P. macrophylla*

27a   leaves short, rigid; scarcely wider than the inflorescence . . . **short-leaved rein orchis**, *P. brevifolia*
27b   leaves otherwise . . . 28

28a   flowers white . . . 29
28b   flowers green to greenish-yellow to creamy green . . . 31

29a   spur greatly exceeding lip in length . . . **Sierra rein orchid**, *P. dilatata* var. *leucostachys*
29b   spur equal to or shorter than lip . . . 30

30a   spur equal to lip in length . . . **tall white northern bog orchis**, *P. dilatata* var. *dilatata*
30b   spur shorter than lip in length . . . **bog candles**, *P. dilatata* var. *albiflora*

31a   spur significantly longer than the lip . . . 32
31b   spur shorter than (or slightly longer than) the lip . . . 34

32a   leaves concentrated on the lower 1/4 of the stem . . . **cloistered bog orchid**, *P. zothecina*
32b   leaves scattered along the stem . . . 33

33a spur filiform; lip linear . . . **Thurber's bog orchid**, *P. limosa*

33b spur thickened, usually scrotiform; lip oblong . . . **few-flowered rein orchis**, *P. sparsiflora*

34a lip rhombic-lanceolate . . . 35

34b lip linear, elliptic, or broadly lanceolate . . . 37

35a lip broadest at base . . . 36

35b lip oblong . . . **slender bog orchis**, *P. stricta*

36a spur saccate or scrotiform . . . **short-spurred bog orchis**, *P. purpurascens*

36b spur clavate or cylindrical . . . 37

37a lip lanceolate; widespread in North America . . . **green bog orchis**, *P. huronensis*

37b lip ovate; Greenland . . . **northern rein orchis**, *P. hyperborea*

note: **lily-leaved rein orchis**, *Platanthera convallariaefolia* may occur in the western Alaskan islands. Identification is difficult and plants previously identified as such in Hultén and Luer are incorrect. See Sheviak in *FNA* for more details.

Key 24

Platythelys

1a longest leaf proportions 4:1; central lobe of the lip cordate; capsule prominently ribbed; plants of central and northern Florida . . . **low ground orchid**, *P. querceticola*

1b longest leaf proportions 6:1; central lobe of the lip rhomboidal; capsule indistinctly ribbed; plants of southern Florida . . . **Cuban ground orchid**, *P. sagreana*

Key 25

Ponthieva

1a petals broad, prominently striped with green . . . **shadow-witch**, *P. racemosa*

1b petals narrow, lacking the green stripe . . . **Mrs. Britton's shadow-witch**, *P. brittoniae*

Key 26

Prosthechea

1a	lip lowermost . . . **Florida dollar orchid**, *P. boothiana* var. *erythronioides*
1b	lip uppermost . . . 2

2a	flowers large, to 4 or 5 cm, green and purple . . . **Florida clamshell orchid**, *P. cochleata* var. *triandra*
2b	flowers very tiny, 2–4 mm, often cleistogamous . . . **dwarf butterfly orchid**, *P. pygmaea*

Key 27

Sacoila

1a	plants with leaves at flowering time . . . **Fakahatchee beaked orchid**, *S. lanceolata* var. *paludicola*
1b	plants leafless at flowering . . . 2

2a	mentum less than 1/3 the length of the perianth; plants puberulent . . . **leafless beaked orchid**, *S. lanceolata* var. *lanceolata*
2b	mentum greater than 1/3, usually greater than 1/2 the length of the perianth; plants scurfy . . . **hoary leafless beaked orchid**, *S. squamulosa*

Key 28

Spiranthes

Note: *Spiranthes cernua* is a compilospecies with gene flow from several other species, depending on the plant's geographic location. Occasionally these plants prove problematic.

1a	leaves somewhat ascending the stem and relatively narrow and grass-like at flowering time . . . 2
1b	leaves otherwise, that is, basal, oval, orbicular, or oblanceolate or absent . . . 20

2a	plants essentially spring flowering (January–May) . . . 3
2b	plants essentially summer or autumn flowering (June–November) . . . 6

3a   flowers white . . . 4
3b   flowers green to creamy green . . . **woodland ladies'-tresses**, *S. sylvatica*

4a   sepals appressed . . . **giant ladies'-tresses**, *S. praecox*
4b   sepals spreading . . . 5

5a   hairs pointed; late winter to spring flowering . . . **grass-leaved ladies'-tresses**, *S. vernalis*
5b   hairs ball-tipped; late spring to summer flowering . . . **lace-lipped ladies'-tresses**, *S. laciniata*

6a   plants essentially summer flowering (June–August) . . . 7
6b   plants essentially autumn flowering (September–November) . . . 16

7a   plants of southern Florida . . . 8
7b   plants of elsewhere . . . 9

8a   margin of lip crenulate . . . **Ames' ladies'-tresses**, *S. amesiana*
8b   margin of lip ciliate-undulate . . . **southern ladies'-tresses**, *S. torta*

9a   lip with a bright yellow central portion . . . **shining ladies'-tresses**, *S. lucida*
9b   lip white or cream-colored . . . 10

10a   lip creamy yellow; usually contrasting with petals and sepals . . . 11
10b   lip same color as petals and sepals . . . 12

11a   hairs long-pointed . . . **grass-leaved ladies'-tresses**, *S. vernalis*
11b   hairs ball-tipped . . . **lace-lipped ladies'-tresses**, *S. laciniata*

12a   flowers ascending, ringent (tubular) . . . **western ladies'-tresses**, *S. porrifolia*
12b   flowers gaping (to some degree) . . . 13

13a   flowers ascending . . . 14
13b   flowers held horizontally; plants of southeastern Arizona . . . **Canelo Hills ladies'-tresses**, *S. delitescens*

14a   petals connivent, forming a hood . . . **hooded ladies'-tresses**, *S. romanzoffiana*
14b   petals otherwise . . . 15

15a   rachis glabrous; minutely farinose; plants of Nye County, Nevada . . . **Ash Meadows ladies'-tresses**, *S. infernalis*

15b   rachis sparsely to densely pubescent; plants of central mountain states . . . **Ute ladies'-tresses**, *S. diluvialis*

16a   plants stoloniferous, usually in damp to wet areas in both sun and shade; inflorescence a dense spike; lip often yellow or greenish . . . **fragrant ladies'-tresses**, *S. odorata*

16b   plants otherwise . . . 17

17a   plants of rich woodlands and second-growth forests; a cauline leaf prominent . . . 18

17b   plants of various habitats, especially fields, meadows, and glades . . . 19

18a   flowers fully sexual, rostellum present; all flowers opening fully and fruit sequentially . . . **southern oval ladies'-tresses**, *S. ovalis* var. *ovalis*

18b   flowers lack a rostellum, therefore self-pollination; frequently not all flowers opening fully; flowers fruit simultaneously . . . **northern oval ladies'-tresses**, *S. ovalis* var. *erostellata*

19a   margins of the lateral sepals distinctly separated from the dorsal sepal; flowers creamy white to nearly straw-colored, with the underside of the lip often a rich butterscotch color . . . **yellow ladies'-tresses**, *S. ochroleuca*

19b   margins of the lateral sepals clearly touching or approximate to the dorsal sepal; flowers milky white to creamy ivory, the center of the lip rarely pale ivory or greenish . . . **nodding ladies'-tresses**, *S. cernua*

20a   plants spring flowering; southeastern United States . . . 21

20b   plants summer and/or autumn flowering . . . 23

21a   flowers white with a green throat . . . **Eaton's ladies'-tresses**, *S. eatonii*

21b   flowers creamy yellow . . . 22

22a   inflorescence essentially glabrous . . . **Florida ladies'-tresses**, *S. floridana*

22b   inflorescence densely pubescent . . . **short-lipped ladies'-tresses**, *S. brevilabris*

23a   plants of southern Florida . . . 24

23b   plants of other areas . . . 25

24a   margin of lip crenulate . . . **Ames' ladies'-tresses,** *S. amesiana*
24b   margin of lip ciliate-undulate . . . **southern ladies'-tresses,** *S. torta*
        (leaves of both species are linear but usually absent or withering at flowering time)

25a   plants essentially summer flowering (June–August) . . . 26
25b   plants essentially autumn flowering (September–November) . . . 28

26a   flowers with green on the lip . . . 27
26b   flowers lacking green on the lip; flowers pure pristine white . . . **little ladies'-tresses,** *S. tuberosa*

27a   flowers laxly arranged on the spike; inflorescence capitate-pubescent; leaves usually persisting through anthesis . . . **northern slender ladies'-tresses,** *S. lacera* var. *lacera*
27b   flowers densely arranged on the spike; entire plant essentially glabrous; leaves usually absent at anthesis . . . **southern slender ladies'-tresses,** *S. lacera* var. *gracilis*

28a   petals with a longitudinal green stripe; plants of east central Texas . . . **Navasota ladies'-tresses,** *S. parksii*
        (leaves are linear but usually absent or withering at flowering time)
28b   flowers otherwise . . . 29

29a   flower entirely white or cream; sepals arching; plants of the prairie habitats . . . **Great Plains ladies'-tresses,** *S. magnicamporum*
29b   flowers white, lip contrasting cream in color; sepals divergent; plants of pine flatwoods and damp roadsides . . . **long-lipped ladies'-tresses,** *S. longilabris*
        (leaves of both species are linear but usually absent or withering at flowering time)

Key 29

Trichocentrum

1a   flowers essentially pink . . . **spread-eagle orchid,** *T. carthagenense*
1b   flower essentially yellow and brown . . . **spotted mule-eared orchid,** *T. undulatum*

Key 30

Triphora

1a	leaves appressed to the stem; inflorescence a corymb . . . **least noddingcaps,** *T. gentianoides*
1b	leaves spreading from the stem; inflorescence other than a corymb . . . 2

2a	leaves essentially green on both surfaces (although some purple may be evident) . . . 3
2b	leaves deep purple on the reverse . . . **Craighead's noddingcaps,** *T. craigheadii*

3a	leaves rounded to heart-shaped; flowers usually more than 1 . . . 4
3b	leaves reniform (kidney-shaped or wider than long); flower always single . . . **wide-leaved noddingcaps,** *T. amazonica*

4a	flowers nodding, white to pink to lavender, fully open; lip lowermost . . . **three birds orchid,** *T. trianthophora* subsp. *trianthophora*
4b	flowers upright, yellow, not fully open; lip uppermost . . . **Rickett's noddingcaps,** *T. rickettii*

Key 31

Vanilla

1a	mature vines leafless . . . 2
1b	mature vines leafy . . . 3

2a	sepals and petals slender, ca. 1 cm wide, 5+ cm long . . . **Dillon's vanilla,** *V. dilloniana*
2b	sepals and petals broad, ca. 1.5 cm wide, less than 5 cm long . . . **worm vine,** *V. barbellata*

3a	leaves longer than the internodes . . . 4
3b	leaves shorter than the internodes . . . **oblong-leaved vanilla,** *V. phaeantha*

4a	sepals and petal margins undulate and tips reflexed . . . **thin-leaved vanilla, scentless vanilla,** *V. mexicana*
4b	sepal and petal margins not undulate . . . 5

5a	lip entire . . . **southern vanilla,** *V. pompona*
5b	lip 3-lobed . . . **commercial vanilla,** *V. planifolia*

Appendix

Excluded Species

Apart from those species listed as misapplied names, the following have been reported in the literature, or by word of mouth, from North America (primarily Florida) and appear to have no supporting documentation, that is, herbarium specimens or substantiated photographs (McCartney, C. *The Palmetto* 17[1] Spring 1997).

Brassavola cordata Lindley
Cattleya spp.
Encyclia hodgeana (A.D. Hawkes) Beckner
Leochilus labiatus Cogniaux *ex* Urban
Maxillaria sanguinea (Rolfe) L.O. Williams *ex* Hodge
Restrepiella ophiocephala (Lindley) Garay & Dunsterville
Spiranthes sinensis (Persoon) Ames
Tetramicra cf. *caniculata* Urban
Triphora trianthophora subsp. *mexicana* (S. Watson) M.E. Medley

Note: ×*Caloarethusa*
Plants appearing to be hybrids of *Calopogon tuberosus* and *Arethusa bulbosa* have been reported from Newfoundland (Pinkepank, H. 1993. "Visiting the Orchids in Newfoundland," *Schlechteriana* 4[1–2]:59–65.) and according to the author are identical with those of the artificially made horticultural hybrid ×*Caloarethusa* Poet's Song made and registered by Robert Yannetti in 1990. The bigeneric name ×*Caloarethusa* has never been published as a botanical name and therefore cannot be used.

Additions, Corrections, Nomenclatural Changes, and Comments for Luer (1972), *The Native Orchids of Florida,* and Luer (1975), *The Native Orchids of the United States and Canada excluding Florida*

For those fortunate enough to own, or have access to a copy of, Carlyle Luer's original works on the orchids of Florida and the orchids of the United States and Canada, the following additions, corrections, and comments are assembled. These in no way should detract from the usefulness of those books, but simply allow for more than 25 years of research and nomenclatural changes as well as for the addition of several species that had not been described as of the date of publication. Names of authors may be found in the text and checklist. No attempt has been made to rework the keys or the index.

The Native Orchids of Florida (1972)

Preface

pp. 8, 9, pl. 1:4 for *Cypripedium calceolus* var. *pubescens* read *Cypripedium parviflorum* var. *pubescens*

Introduction

pp. 22, 23, pl. 4:8 for *Oncidium luridum* read *Trichocentrum undulatum*

Key

pp. 24, 25, pl. 5:8 *Calopogon tuberosus* var. *simpsonii* forma *niveus*
p. 28 couplet 14 for *Centrogenium* read *Eltroplectris*
p. 29 couplet 31 contains all of the *Spiranthes* segregate genera
p. 30 couplet 41a for *Eulophia* read *Eulophia, Pteroglossaspis*
p. 31 couplet 52 for *Erythrodes* read *Platythelys*
p. 31 couplet 57a for *Polyrrhiza* read *Dendrophylax*
p. 31 couplet 61a for *Encyclia* read *Encyclia* & *Prosthechea*

p. 32 couplet 65a for *Oncidium* read *Trichocentrum*

p. 34 couplet 69a for *Oncidium* read *Oncidium* & *Tolumnia*

Text

pp. 38, 39, pl. 6:5 forma *albiflora*

pp. 42, 43, pl. 8:6 forma *leucantha*

pp. 50, 51 for *Triphora latifolia* read *Triphora amazonica*

pp. 58, 59, pl. 15:8 *albiflora*

pp. 62, 63, pl. 16:1,6 forma *albiflorus*

pp. 66, 67, pl. 17:6 forma *viridis*

pp. 73, 74, pl. 19:3,4 for *Vanilla inodora* read *Vanilla mexicana*

pp. 82, 86, 87, pl. 22:1,2 for *Ponthieva racemosa* var. *brittonae* read *Ponthieva brittoniae*

p. 90 couplet 6a for *Spiranthes tortilis* read *Spiranthes torta*

p. 90 couplet 8a for *Spiranthes grayi* read *Spiranthes tuberosa*

p. 90 couplet 10 for *Spiranthes brevilabris* var. *brevilabris* read *Spiranthes brevilabris*

p. 90 couplet 10a for *Spiranthes brevilabris* var. *floridana* read *Spiranthes floridana*

p. 90 couplet 12a for *Spiranthes cernua* var. *odorata* read *Spiranthes odorata*

p. 91 couplet 15a for *S. polyantha* read *Mesadenus lucayanus*

p. 91 couplet 16 for *S. costaricensis* read *Beloglottis costaricensis*

p. 91 couplet 17 for *S. cranichoides* read *Cyclopogon cranichoides*

p. 91 couplet 17a for *S. elata* read *Cyclopogon elatus*

p. 91 couplet 18a for *S. lanceolata* var. *paludicola* read *Sacoila lanceolata* var. *paludicola*

p. 91 couplet 19 for *S. lanceolata* var. *lanceolata* read *Sacoila lanceolata* var. *lanceolata*

p. 91 couplet 19a for *S. lanceolata* var. *luteoalba* read *Sacoila lanceolata* forma *albidaviridis*

pp. 99, 100, 101, pl. 26:1–5 for *Spiranthes tortilis* read *Spiranthes torta*

pp. 100, 101, pl. 26:6–9 for *Spiranthes gracilis* read *Spiranthes lacera* var. *gracilis*. None of the examples is from Florida; this species is not present in Florida

pp. 102, 103, pl. 27:1–6 for *Spiranthes brevilabris* var. *brevilabris* read *Spiranthes brevilabris*

pp. 102, 104, pl. 28:7–9 for *Spiranthes brevilabris* var. *floridana* read *Spiranthes floridana*

pp. 105, 106, pl. 28:1–5 for *Spiranthes grayi* read *Spiranthes tuberosa*

pp. 108, 109, pl. 29:1 *Spiranthes cernua* is not in Florida

p. 109, pl. 29:2–5 are *Spiranthes odorata;* 6–8 for *Spiranthes cernua* var. *odorata* read *Spiranthes odorata*

p. 110 *Spiranthes cernua* var. *odorata* read *Spiranthes odorata*

p. 111 *Spiranthes cranichoides* read *Cyclopogon cranichoides* pp. 112, 113, pl. 30:1–5 read *Cyclopogon cranichoides;* 6–8 read *Cyclopogon elatus*

pp. 114, 115, pl. 31:1–4 for *Spiranthes costaricensis* read *Beloglottis costaricensis*

pp. 115, 116, pl. 31:5–8 for *Spiranthes polyantha* read *Mesadenus lucayanus*

pp. 117, 118, 119, pl. 32 for *Spiranthes lanceolata* var. *lanceolata* read *Sacoila lanceolata* var. *lanceolata*

pp. 120, 121, pl. 33 for *Spiranthes lanceolata* var. *luteoalba* read *Sacoila lanceolata* forma *albidaviridis;* for *Spiranthes lanceolata* var. *paludicola* read *Sacoila lanceolata* var. *paludicola*

p. 121, pl. 33:1–3 read *Sacoila lanceolata;* 4–6 read *Sacoila lanceolata* forma *albidaviridis;* 7–9 read *Sacoila lanceolata* var. *paludicola*

pp. 123, 124, pl. 34 *Centrogenium setaceum* read *Eltroplectris calcarata*

p. 126, pl. 35:1,2,4,6 for *Erythrodes querceticola* read *Platythelys querceticola;* 3,5 read *Platythelys sagreana* (no description of *P. sagreana,* but a reference on p. 128 to var. *sagreana*)

pp. 142, 143, pl.40:3 for *P.* ×*chapmanii* read *P. chapmanii;* 7 for *P.* ×*canbyi* read *P.* ×*channellii*

p. 151 for *Platanthera* ×*chapmanii* read *Platanthera chapmanii* and delete the hybrid combination of *P. ciliaris* × *P. cristata*

pp. 153, 156, 157, pl. 45:3,4,5, p. 158 for *Habenaria quinqueseta* var. *macroceratitis* read *Habenaria macroceratitis*

pp. 174, 175, pl. 51 read forma *albolabia*

pp. 184, pl. 54:5–7, 186, 187 *Restrepiella* is not found in Florida

pp. 191, 192, 193, pl. 56:2–5 *Tetramicra* is not found in Florida

p. 195 couplet 2a, 3, 3a for *Encyclia* read *Prosthechea*

pp. 198, 199, pl. 55:5 read forma *albolabia*

pp. 200, 202 for *Encyclia* read *Prosthechea*

p. 203, pl. 60:8 *Prosthechea cochleata* var. *triandra* forma *albidoflava*

p. 204 for *Encyclia* read *Prosthechea*

p. 208 for *Epidendrum conopseum* read *Epidendrum magnoliae*

p. 210 for *Epidendrum anceps* read *Epidendrum amphistomum*

pp. 210, 211, pl. 63:1 forma *rubrifolium*

p. 212 for *Epidendrum difforme* read *Epidendrum floridense*

pp. 221, 222, p. 68 for *Polystachya flavescens* read *Polystachya concreta*

pp. 232, 233, pl. 71:1,2, p. 234 for *Cyrtopodium andersonii* read *Cyrtopodium polyphyllum*

p. 236 couplet 1a for *Eulophia ecristata* read *Pteroglossaspis ecristata*

p. 238, pl. 72:6 for albino form read forma *pallida*

p. 240 for *Eulophia ecristata* read *Pteroglossaspis ecristata*

p. 243 for *Govenia utriculata* read *Govenia floridana*

p. 244 for *Galeandra beyrichii* read *Galeandra bicarinata*

p. 244, captions for p. 245, pl. 74:1,2 *Govenia floridana;* 3,4 *Govenia utriculata;* 5–8 *Galeandra bicarinata*

pp. 255, 256, 257, pl. 77 for *Oncidium bahamense* read *Tolumnia bahamensis*

p. 255 couplet 3 for *Oncidium luridum* read *Trichocentrum undulatum*

p. 255 couplet 3a for *Oncidium carthagenense* read *Trichocentrum carthagenense*

pp. 258, 259, pl. 78:6,7 for *Oncidium carthagenense* read *Trichocentrum carthagenense*

p. 260 for *Oncidium luridum* read *Trichocentrum undulatum;* pl. 78:6 forma *flavovirens;* 7 Trichocentrum *luridum*

p. 262 for *Oncidium carthagenense* read *Trichocentrum carthagenense*

pp. 263, 264, pl. 80:1,2 *Leochilus* is not found in Florida

pp. 277, 278, pl. 84 *Polyrrhiza* read *Dendrophylax*

for *Spathoglottis plicata* see *Native Orchids of the United States and Canada excluding Florida,* pp. 280, 281, 286, pl. 78:5,6

The following taxa are not treated in *The Native Orchids of Florida*

Bletia florida

Bletilla striata

Encyclia rufa

Epidendrum radicans

Laelia rubescens

Maxillaria parviflora

Oeceoclades maculata

Pelexia adnata

Phaius tankervillae

Platythelys sagreana

Sacoila squamulosa

Spathoglottis plicata

Spiranthes amesiana

Spiranthes eatonii

Spiranthes ovalis var. *erostellata*

Spiranthes sylvatica

Vanilla pompona

Hybrids:

Platanthera ×*channellii*

Spiranthes ×*folsomii*

Spiranthes ×*itchetuckneensis*

Spiranthes ×*meridionalis*

The Native Orchids of the United States and Canada excluding Florida (1975)

Introduction

p. 11 for *Dactylorhiza maculata* read *Dactylorhiza majalis* (Reichenbach) P.F. Hunt & Summerhayes var. *junialis* (Vermeulen) Senghas

p. 12 for *Cypripedium calceolus* var. *planipetalum* read *Cypripedium parviflorum* var. *pubescens* extreme form; *Calopogon tuberosus* var. *latifolius* and var. *nanus* read dwarf forms; *P. hookeri* var. *abbreviata* read *P. hookeri* forma *abbreviata; P. obtusata* var. *collecteana* read *P. obtusata* forma *collecteana; P. orbiculata* var. *lehorsii* read *P. orbiculata* forma *lehorsii*; for *Cypripedium calceolus* var. *pubescens* read *Cypripedium parviflorum* var. *pubescens*; for *Malaxis monophyllos* var. *brachypoda* read *Malaxis brachypoda*; for *Platanthera hyperborea* read *Platanthera aquilonis*

p. 16 for *Polyrrhiza lindenii* read *Dendrophylax lindenii*

p. 32 for *Polyradicion* read *Dendrophylax*

Text

p. 39 couplets 7 & 8 see *Cypripedium* key in text on page 168; for couplet 13a for *C. guttatum* var. *yatabeanum* read *C. yatabeanum*

pp. 40, 41, pl. 1:3,4 forma albiflorum

pp. 42, 43, pl. 2:1 forma albiflorum

p. 44 for *Cypripedium calceolus* Linnaeus var. *pubescens* (Willdenow) Correll read *Cypripedium parviflorum* Salisbury var. *pubescens* (Willdenow) Knight

pp. 44, 45, pl. 3, p. 46, 47, pl. 4 for *Cypripedium calceolus* var. *pubescens* read *Cypripedium parviflorum* var. *pubescens*

p. 48 for *Cypripedium calceolus* Linnaeus var. *parviflorum* Salisbury read *Cypripedium parviflorum* Salisbury var. *makasin* (Farwell) Sheviak

p. 49 for *Cypripedium* ×*andrewsii* Fuller read *Cypripedium* ×*andrewsii* Fuller nm. *andrewsii*; for *Cypripedium* ×*favillianum* Curtis read *C.* ×*andrewsii* Fuller nm. *favillianum* (Curtis) Boivin; *C. calceolus* var. *parviflorum* read *Cypripedium parviflorum* var. *makasin*; for *C.* ×*landonii* read *C.* ×*andrewsii* nm. *landonii*

pp. 50, 51, pl. 5:1,2 for *Cypripedium calceolus* var. *parviflorum* read *Cypripedium parviflorum* var. *makasin*; pl. 5:3,4,5, for *Cypripedium calceolus* Linnaeus var. *planipetalum* (Fernald) Victorin & Rousseau read *C. parviflorum* var. *pubescens* extreme expression

pp. 52, 53, pl. 6:5 read *Cypripedium* ×*andrewsii* nm. *favillianum;* pl. 6:6 read *Cypripedium* × *andrewsii* nm. *andrewsii*

pp. 56, 57, pl. 8:5 for (*Cypripedium album*) read forma *albiflorum*

p. 66 for *Cypripedium guttatum* var. *guttatum* read *Cypripedium guttatum*

p. 67, pl. 13:1–5 for *Cypripedium guttatum* var. *guttatum* read *Cypripedium guttatum;* 6–7 for *Cypripedium guttatum* var. *yatabeanum* read *Cypripedium yatabeanum*

p. 68 for *Cypripedium guttatum* Swartz var. *yatabeanum* (Makino) Pfitzer read *Cypripedium yatabeanum* Makino

p. 72 for *austinae* read *austiniae*

pp. 76, 77, pl 15:3 forma *viridens*

pp. 82, 83, pl. 17:5 forma *viridis*

pp. 84, 85, pl. 18:4 forma *viridens*

p. 99 couplet 6a for *S. graminea* read *S. delitescens;* couplet 7a for *S. tortilis* read *S. torta;* couplet 10a for *S. intermedia* read *S. casei;* couplet 14a for *S. brevilabris* var. *floridana* read *S. floridana*

p. 100 couplet 20 for *S. intermedia* read *S. casei;* couplet 21a for 16. *S. graminea* read *S. delitescens;* couplet 29 for *S. cranichoides* read *Cyclopogon cranichoides;* couplet 30 for *S. elata* read *Cyclopogon elatus;* couplet 30a for *S. parasitica* read *Schiedeella arizonica;* 28a for *S. costaricensis* read *Beloglottis costaricensis;* couplet 27a for *S. polyantha* read *Mesadenus lucayanus*

p. 101 couplet 33 for *S. durangensis* read *Deiregyne confusa;* couplet 33a for *S. michuacana* read *Stenorrhynchos michuacanum;* couplet 34 for *S. lanceolata* read *Sacoila lanceolata;* couplet 34a for *S. lanceolata* var. *luteoalba* read *Sacoila lanceolata* var. *lanceolata* forma *albidaviridis;* couplet 35 for *S. lanceolata* var. *paludicola* read *Sacoila lanceolata* var. *paludicola;* couplet 35a for *S. cinnabarina* read *Dichromanthus cinnabarinus*

p. 102 (chart) for *brevilabris* var. *brevilabris* read *brevilabris;* for *brevilabris* var. *floridana* read *floridana;* for *graminea* read *delitescens;* for *tortilis* read *torta*

p. 105, pl. 22:5 forma *albolabia*

p. 106 for *Spiranthes intermedia* read *Spiranthes casei* var. *casei*

p. 107, pl. 23:3–5 *Spiranthes casei* var. *casei*

p. 108 for *Spiranthes intermedia* Ames read *Spiranthes casei* Catling & Cruise var. *casei*

p. 114 read var. *ovalis*

pp. 124, 125, pl. 28:6 delete *Spiranthes* ×*steigeri*

p. 126 delete ×*steigeri*

p. 127 for *Spiranthes graminea* Lindley read *Spiranthes delitescens* Sheviak

p. 128 for *Spiranthes parasitica* A. Richard & Galeotti read *Schiedeella arizonica* P.M. Brown

pp. 128, 129, pl. 29:1–3 for *Spiranthes graminea* read *Spiranthes delitescens;* 5–9 for *Spiranthes parasitica* read *Schiedeella arizonica* pp. 130, 131, pl. 30 for *Spiranthes durangensis* Ames & Schweinfurth read *Deiregyne confusa* Garay

pp. 132, 133, pl. 31:1–3 for *Spiranthes cinnabarina* (Lexarza) Hemsley read *Dichromanthus cinnabarinus* (Lexarza) Garay

pp. 132, 133, pl. 31:4–6, p. 134 for *Spiranthes michuacana* (Lexarza) Hemsley read *Stenorrhynchos michuacanum* (Llave & Lexarza) Lindley

pp. 142, 143, pl. 34:5 forma *reticulata*

pp. 144, 145, pl 35:7 forma *ophioides*

pp. 148, 149, pl. 36:4 forma *willeyi;* 5 forma *gordinierii;* for *Cypripedium calceolus* var. *pubescens* read *Cypripedium parviflorum* var. *pubescens*

pp. 153, 153, pl. 37:4 forma *lineata*

p. 155 couplet 1a for *D. maculata* read *D. majalis* var. *junialis*

pp. 158, 159, pl. 39:2 forma *alba;* 8,9 for *Dactylorhiza maculata* read *Dactylorhiza majalis* var. *junialis*

p. 160 for *Dactylorhiza maculata* (Linnaeus) Soo read *Dactylorhiza majalis* (Reichenbach) P.F. Hunt & Summerhayes var. *junialis* (Vermeulen) Senghas

p. 163 couplet 2 for *P. elegans* var. *elata* read *P. elongata*

pp. 164, 165, pl. 40:7–9 for *Piperia elegans* var. *elata* read *Piperia elongata*

p. 167 for *Piperia elegans* (Lindley) Rydberg var. *elata* (Jepson) Luer read *Piperia elongata* Rydberg

pp. 168, 169 for *Piperia maritima* Rydberg read *Piperia elegans* (Lindley) Rydberg

p. 177 couplet 9 for *P. ×chapmanii* read *P. chapmanii*

p. 178 couplet 13a for *P. lacera* var. *terrae-novae* read *P. ×andrewsii;* couplet 16 for *P. albida* var. *straminea* read *Pseudorchis straminea;* couplet 22 for *P. orbiculata* var. *orbiculata* read *P. orbiculata;* couplet 23 for *P. orbiculata* var. *macrophylla* read *P. macrophylla*

p. 179 couplet 36 for *P. hyperborea* var. *hyperborea* read *P. aquilonis;* couplet 36a for *P. hyperborea* var. *gracilis* read *P. huronensis;* couplet 37 for *P. hyperborea* var. *huronensis* read *P. huronensis;* couplet 37a for *P. hyperborea* var. *viridiflora* read *P. huronensis;* couplet 34a for *P. ×media* read *P. huronensis;* couplet 39 for *P. hyperborea* var. *purpurascens* read *P. purpurascens;* couplet 35 for *P. sparsiflora* var. *brevifolia* read *P. brevifolia*

p. 187 for *P. ×chapmanii* (Small) Luer read *P. chapmanii* (Small) Luer *emend.* Folsom

pp. 188, 189, pl.46:4,6 for *P. ×chapmanii* read *P. chapmanii*

pp. 192, 193, pl. 48:8,9 for *Platanthera lacera* var. *terrae-novae* read *P. ×andrewsii*

p. 194 for *Platanthera lacera* (Michaux) Don var. *terrae-novae* (Fernald) Luer read *P. ×andrewsii* (White *ex* Niles) Luer

pp. 196, 197, pl. 49:8 forma *albiflora*

pp. 210, 211 for *Platanthera albida* (Linnaeus) Lindley var. *straminea* (Fernald) Luer read *Pseudorchis straminea* (Fernald) Soo; pl. 55:4 for *Platanthera albida* read

Pseudorchis albida; 5–7 for *Platanthera albida* var. *straminea* read *Platanthera straminea*

p. 215 for *Platanthera obtusata* var. *collectanea* read forma *collectanea*

p. 218 for *Platanthera hookeri* var. *abbreviata* read forma *abbreviata*

pp. 220, 221, pl. 59:1,2 for *Platanthera orbiculata* var. *orbiculata* read *Platanthera orbiculata;* 3–4 for *Platanthera orbiculata* var. *macrophylla* read *Platanthera macrophylla*

p. 222 for *Platanthera orbiculata* (Pursh) Lindley var. *macrophylla* (Goldie) Luer read *Platanthera macrophylla* (Goldie) P.M. Brown

p. 228 for *Platanthera hyperborea* (Linnaeus) Lindley var. *hyperborea* read *Platanthera aquilonis* Sheviak

p. 229 for *P.* ×*media* (Rydberg) Luer read *P. huronensis* (Nuttall) Lindley

pp. 230, 231, for *Platanthera hyperborea* (Linnaeus) Lindley var. *huronensis* read *Platanthera huronensis* (Nuttall) Lindley; pl. 61:1,3,4 read *Platanthera aquilonis;* 5–8 read *Platanthera huronensis*

p. 232 for *Platanthera hyperborea* (Linnaeus) Lindley var. *gracilis* (Lindley) Luer read *Platanthera huronensis* (Nuttall) Lindley

p. 233 for *Platanthera hyperborea* (Linnaeus) Lindley var. *viridiflora* (Chamisso) Luer read *Platanthera huronensis* (Nuttall) Lindley

p. 234 for *Platanthera hyperborea* (Linnaeus) Lindley var. *purpurascens* (Rydberg) Luer read *Platanthera purpurascens* (Rydberg) Sheviak & Jennings

pp. 234, 235, pl. 62:1–5 read *Platanthera huronensis;* 6–9 *Platanthera purpurascens*

pp. 240, 241, pl. 64:4–6 for *Platanthera sparsiflora* (S. Watson) Schlechter var. *brevifolia* (Greene) Luer read *Platanthera brevifolia* (Greene) Kranzlin

pp. 246, 247, pl. 66:3,5 forma *leucantha;* 4 for var. *bifaria* read *Cleistes bifaria*

p. 248 for var. *bifaria* read *Cleistes bifaria*

p. 256 for *T. latifolia* read *T. amazonica*

pp. 260, 261, pl. 70:3 forma *albiflorus*

pp. 266, 267, pl. 73:4 forma *albiflora;* 5 forma *subcaerulea*

pp. 270, 271, pl. 74:1 forma *albolabia*

p. 291 couplet 4a for *M. monophyllos* var. *brachypoda* read *M. brachypoda;* couplet 5a for *M. ehrenbergii* read *M. porphyrea;* couplet 6 for *M. tenuis* read *M. abieticola;* couplet 6a for *M. macrostachya* read *M. soulei;* couplet 7a for *M. monophyllos* var. *diphyllos* read *M. diphyllos*

p. 296 for *Spiranthes parasitica* read *Schiedeella arizonica;* for *Platanthera sparsiflora* var. *brevifolia* read *Platanthera brevifolia;* for *M. monophyllos* var. *brachypoda* read *M. brachypoda*

pp. 296, 297, pl. 81 for *Malaxis ehrenbergii* (Reichenbach f.) Kuntze read *Malaxis porphyrea* (Ridley) Kuntze; for *Malaxis ehrenbergii* read *Malaxis porphyrea* pp. 298, 299, pl. 82 for *Malaxis tenuis* (S. Watson) Ames read *Malaxis abieticola* Salazar & Soto Arenas

pp. 300, 301 for *Malaxis macrostachya* (Lexarza) Kuntze read *Malaxis soulei* L.O. Williams

pp. 304, 305, pl. 85:2,3 for *Malaxis monophyllos* (Linnaeus) Swartz var. *brachypoda* (A. Gray) Morris & Ames read *Malaxis brachypoda* (A. Gray) Fernald; 4,5 for *Malaxis monophyllos* var. *diphyllos* read *Malaxis diphyllos*

p. 306 for *Malaxis monophyllos* (Linnaeus) Swartz var. *diphyllos* (Chamisso) Luer read *Malaxis diphyllos* Chamisso

pp. 318, 319, pl. 89:1,9 *Corallorhiza maculata* var. *occidentalis* forma *immaculata*

pp. 320, 321, pl. 90:3 forma *albolabia*

pp. 324, 325, pl. 92:4 forma *eburnea*

pp. 338, 339, pl. 96 forma *albiflora*

The following are not treated in *The Native Orchids of the United States and Canada excluding Florida*

Calopogon oklahomensis

Corallorhiza maculata var. *mexicana*

Corallorhiza maculata var. *occidentalis*

Corallorhiza odontorhiza var. *pringlei*

Cypripedium kentuckiense

Cypripedium parviflorum var. *parviflorum*

Dactylorhiza majalis subsp. *praetermissa*

Epipactis atrorubens

Hexalectris spicata var. *arizonica*

Piperia candida

Piperia colemanii

Piperia cooperi

Piperia elegans subsp. *decurtata*

Piperia leptopetala

Piperia transversa

Piperia yadonii

Platanthera pallida

Platanthera zothecina

Spiranthes casei var. *novaescotiae*

Spiranthes diluvialis

Spiranthes eatonii

Spiranthes infernalis

Spiranthes ovalis var. *erostellata*

Spiranthes sylvatica

Hybrids:

Cypripedium ×*alaskanum*
Cypripedium ×*columbianum*
Liparis ×*jonesii*
Listera ×*veltmanii*
Platanthera ×*channellii*
Platanthera ×*correllii*
Platanthera ×*estesii*
Platanthera ×*hollandiae*
Platanthera ×*kennanii*
Platanthera ×*lassenii*
Platanthera ×*reznicekii*
Platanthera ×*vossii*
Spiranthes ×*borealis*
Spiranthes ×*folsomii*
Spiranthes ×*itchetuckneensis*
Spiranthes ×*intermedia*
Spiranthes ×*meridionalis*
Spiranthes ×*simpsonii*

Glossary

adventive: non-native

amphidiploid: a species resulting from the hybridization of two diploid species

anterior: front or upper

anthesis: time of flowering

appressed: placed tightly against; opposite of divergent

auricle: with ear-like appendages

axillary: on the side

basal rosette: a cluster of leaves all arising at the base of the plant

bract: a modified leaf

calcareous: limy

calciphile: a lime lover

capitate: like a head; "with capitate hairs" refers to hairs with ball-like tips

cauline: on the stem

chasmogamous: with fully open, usually sexual flowers

chlorophyll: the green substance manufactured by the plant

cilate: with short, slender hairs

circumneutral: a pH of about 6.5

clavate: club-shaped

cleistogamous: with closed flowers that are usually self-pollinating

cordate: heart-shaped

coriaceous: leathery

corymb: a determinate inflorescence where all of the branches are the same length and the outer flowers open first

crenulate: with a short, wavy margin

crest: a series of ridges or a group of hairs; usually yellow or a color contrasting with the lip

cyme: a determinate inflorescence with central flowers opening first

determinate: with a specific ending, not continuing to grow indefinitely

distal: the further away or the underside

divergent: spreading or widely separated

dorsal sepal: the sepal opposite the lip; usually uppermost in most orchids

emarginate: with a short projection at the tip

endemic: native to a specific area

ephemeral: short-lived; often a few weeks each season

epiphyte, epiphytic: living in the air

erose: with an irregular margin

extant: still to be found

extirpated: no longer to be found

farinose: mealy

filiform: slender and threadlike

glabrous: smooth

glaucous: with a whitish cast

habit: the way a plant grows

habitat: where a plant grows

hemi-epiphyte: usually growing on the base of trees or on logs

hoary: with white scales

isthmus: a narrowed portion between the apex and base of the lip

keel: a ridge

lacerate: slashed

lateral sepals: the sepals positioned on the side of the flower

lip: the modified third petal of an orchid

marl: a calcareous or limy wetland

mentum: a short, rounded, thickened projection formed by the petals; similar to a spur but not tapered to a point

mesic: of medium conditions

naturalized: a non-native species that is reproducing in its adopted habitat

nominate, nominate variety: the pure species, exclusive of subspecies, variety, or form

non-resupinate: with only a single twist so the lip is at the top

oblanceolate: narrowly oblong

obovate: broadly oblong

orifice: opening

ovary: the female structure that produces the seed

panicle: a branching inflorescence similar to a raceme; the flowers stalked

papillose: with fine raised dots

pedicellate flowers: those flowers held on pedicel or stalks

pedicellate ovary: typically the ovary of an orchid flower where the ovary and the flower stalk appear to merge into one structure

peduncle: the stalk of a flower or leaf

petiole: the stem portion of the leaf

plicate: soft and with many longitudinal ribs, often folded

posterior: lower or rear

pseudobulb: a swollen storage organ that is prominent in many epiphytic orchids and occasionally in a few genera of terrestrial orchids

puberulent: with a fine dusting of very short, soft hairs

pubescent, pubescence: downy with short, soft hairs

raceme: an unbranched, indeterminate inflorescence with stalked flowers; branched racemes are technically panicles

reniform: kidney-shaped

resupinate: twisted around so that the lip is lowermost

rhombic: with parallel sides but then tapered on both ends

ringent: gaping

saccate: sack-shaped

scape: a leafless stem that arises from the base of the plant

scrotiform: saccate but with two pouches

secund: all to one side

segregate (species), segregate genus: a genus that has been separated from another larger genus

sepals: the outer floral envelope

serpentine: a geologic formation of high metal minerals such as nickel and magnesium; few plants grow here and they are usually very specialized

serpentiphile: lover of serpentine

sessile: without a stem or stalk

spatulate: oblong with a narrowed base

spike: an unbranched inflorescence with sessile or unstalked flowers

spiranthoid: a *Spiranthes* or member of a genus closely allied to *Spiranthes*

spur: a slender tubular or sac-like structure usually formed at the base of the lip, and often containing nectar

striate: with stripes

taxa: species, subspecies, variety, form

terete: rounded

terminal: at the end

transverse: growing horizontal (as opposed to parallel) to the axis (or stem)

tubercle: a thickened projection

twig epiphyte: living on slender twigs, often at the periphery of the host

umbel: an inflorescence where the flower stems all arise from the same point like the spokes of an umbrella

undulate: wavy

waif: applied to a random individual occurrence

whorl: all coming from the same point on the axis in a circular pattern

Bibliography

Note: In addition to the references with many of the species, this list includes all of the local, regional, and national orchid floras for North America, north of Mexico. It also includes several other general references that will be helpful. The many comprehensive regional floras would also be useful, all of which include the Orchidaceae.

Ackerman, J.D. "An Orchid Flora of Puerto Rico and the Virgin Islands." *Memoirs.* Vol. 73. Bronx: New York Botanical Garden, 1995.

Ames, B. *Drawings of Florida Orchids.* Cambridge, Mass.: Botanical Museum of Harvard University, 1947.

Ames, O. *A Contribution to Our Knowledge of the Orchid Flora of Southern Florida.* North Easton, Mass.: Ames Botanical Laboratory, 1904.

———. *Orchidaceae.* Vol. 4, *The Genus Habenaria in North America.* North Easton, Mass.: Ames Botanical Laboratory, 1910.

———. *An Enumeration of the Orchids of the United States and Canada.* Boston: American Orchid Society, 1924.

Baldwin, H. *The Orchids of New England.* New York: John Wiley & Sons, 1884.

Bentley, S.L. *Native Orchids of the Southern Appalachian Mountains.* Chapel Hill: University of North Carolina Press, 2000.

Bingham, M.T. *Orchids of Michigan.* Bloomfield Hills, Mich.: Cranbrook Institute of Science, 1939.

Brown, P.M. *A Field and Study Guide to the Orchids of New England and New York.* Jamaica Plain, Mass.: Orchis Press, 1993.

Brown, P.M., and S.N. Folsom. *Wild Orchids of the Northeastern United States.* Ithaca, N.Y.: Cornell University Press, 1997.

———. *Wild Orchids of Florida.* Gainesville: University Press of Florida, 2002.

Bruce-Grey Plant Committee. *The Orchids of Bruce and Grey* (Counties, Ontario). Owen Sound, Ont.: Stan Brown, 1997.

Burian, R. *Native Orchids of Oregon.* Portland: Oregon Orchid Society, 2000.

Busswell, W. "Native Orchids of South Florida." *Bulletin of the University of Miami* 19, no. 3 (1945): 3–29.

Cameron, J.W. *The Orchids of Maine.* Orono: University of Maine at Orono, 1976.

Case, F.W. *Orchids of the Western Great Lakes Region.* Rev. ed., Bulletin 48. Bloomfield Hills, Mich.: Cranbrook Institute of Science, 1987.

Catling, P.M. "Biology of North American Representatives of the Subfamily Spiran-thoideae," in *North American Native Terrestrial Orchid Propagation and Production*. Chadds Ford, Pa.: Brandywine Conservancy, 1989.

Chapman, W.K. *Orchids of the Northeast*. Syracuse, N.Y.: Syracuse University Press, 1997.

Coleman, R.A. *The Wild Orchids of California*. Ithaca, N.Y.: Cornell University Press, 1995.

———. *The Wild Orchids of Arizona and New Mexico*. Ithaca, N.Y.: Cornell University Press, 2002.

Correll, D.S. *Native Orchids of North America*. Waltham, Mass.: Chronica Botanica, 1950.

Craighead, F.C. *Orchids and Other Air Plants of Everglades National Park*. Coral Gables, Fla.: University of Miami Press, 1963.

Cribb, P. *The Genus Cypripedium*. Portland, Oreg.: Timber Press, 1997.

Donly, J.F. *The Orchids of Nova Scotia*. Privately published, 1963.

Ettman, J.K., and D.R. McAdoo. *An Annotated Catalogue and Distribution Account of the Kentucky Orchidaceae*. Louisville: The Kentucky Society of Natural History Charitable Trust, 1979.

Fisher, R.M. *The Orchids of the Cypress Hills*. Privately published, 1980.

Flora of North America Editorial Committee, eds. *Flora of North America North of Mexico*. 5+ vols. New York and Oxford: Oxford University Press, 1993–.

Fuller, A. "Studies on the Flora of Wisconsin. Part 1: The Orchids; Orchidaceae." *Bulletin of the Public Museum of Milwaukee* 14, no. 1 (1933): 1–248.

Garay, L.A. "A Generic Revision of the Spiranthinae." *Botanical Museum Leaflet, Harvard University* 28, no. 4 (1982): 277–425.

Gibson, W.H. *Our Native Orchids*. New York: Doubleday, Page and Company, 1905.

Gupton, O.W., and F.C. Swope. *Wild Orchids of the Middle Atlantic States*. Knoxville: University of Tennessee Press, 1986.

Hammer, R. "A Status Report on the Native and Naturalized Orchidaceae of Collier, Miami-Dade and Monroe Counties, Florida." *North American Native Orchid Journal* 7, no. 1 (March 2001): 3–84.

Haperman, J. *Orchids of Wisconsin*. Madison: Wisconsin State Herbarium, University of Wisconsin–Madison, 2000. CD-ROM format.

Henry, L.K., W.E. Buker, and D.L. Pearth. "Western Pennsylvania Orchids." *Castanea* 40, no. 2 (1975): 93–168. Pittsburgh, Pa.: Carnegie Museum of Natural History.

Homoya, M.A. *Orchids of Indiana*. Bloomington and Indianapolis: Indiana Academy of Science, Indiana University Press, 1993.

Kartesz, J.T. *A Synonymized Checklist of the Vascular Flora of the United States, Canada, and Greenland*. 3d ed. Chapel Hill: North Carolina Botanical Garden, 2000.

Keenan, P.E. *A Complete Guide to Maine's Orchids*. Freeport, Maine: DeLorme Publishing Company, 1983.

———. *Wild Orchids across North America*. Portland, Oreg.: Timber Press, 1999.

Lamont, E.E. "Atlas of the Orchids of Long Island, New York." *Bulletin of the Torrey Botanical Club* 123 (1996): 157–66.

Lamont, E.E., J.M. Beitel, and R.E. Zaremba. "Current Status of Orchids on Long Island." *Torreya* 115, no. 2 (1988): 113–21.

Liggo, J., and A.O. Liggo. *Wild Orchids of Texas*. Austin: University of Texas Press, 1999.

Long, J.C. *Native Orchids of Colorado.* Museum Pictorial 16. Denver, Colo.: Denver Museum of Natural History, 1970.

Luer, C.A. *The Native Orchids of Florida.* Bronx: New York Botanical Garden, 1972.

———. *The Native Orchids of the United States and Canada excluding Florida.* Bronx: New York Botanical Garden, 1975.

McCartney, C.L., Jr. *A Thrice Annotated Checklist of the Orchids of Southeastern Florida.* Rev. ed.. Hollywood, Fla.: Published privately, 1987.

Morris, F., and E. Eames. *Our Wild Orchids.* New York: Charles Scribner's Sons, 1929.

Munden, C. *Native Orchids of Nova Scotia.* Sydney, Nova Scotia: University College of Cape Breton Press, 2001.

Niles, G.G. *Bog Trotting for Orchids.* New York: G.P. Putnam's Sons, 1904.

Nir, M. *Orchidaceae Antillanae.* New York: DAG Publishing, 2000.

Nylander, O.O. *Orchids of Northern Maine.* Presque Isle, Maine: Star-Herald Publishing Co., 1935.

Petrie, W. *Guide to the Orchids of North America.* Blaine, Wash.: Hancock House, 1981.

Reddoch, J.M., and A. Reddoch. "The Orchids of the Ottawa District." *Canadian Field-Naturalist* 111, no. 1 (January–March 1997): 1–186.

Salazar, M.A., M. Chase, and M.A. Soto Arenas. 2002. *Lindleyana* 17 (3): 173.

Schrenk, W.J. "Zussammenstellung der Orchideenarten der Vereinigten Staaten von Amerika und der amerikanishen Jungferninsein." (Compilation of the Orchid Species of the United States of America and the Virgin Islands [belonging to the U.S.]). *Die Orchidee* 28 (1977): 98–104.

Sheviak, C.J. *An Introduction to the Ecology of the Illinois Orchidaceae.* Springfield: Illinois State Museum, 1974.

———. *Biosystematic Study of the Spiranthes cernua Complex.* Bulletin 448. Albany: New York State Museum, 1982.

Slaughter, C.R. *Wild Orchids of Arkansas.* Morrilton, Ark.: Privately published, 1993.

Smith, W.R. *Orchids of Minnesota.* Minneapolis: University of Minnesota Press, 1993.

Smreciu, E.A., and R.S. Currah. *A Guide to the Native Orchids of Alberta.* Edmonton: University of Alberta Devonian Botanical Garden, 1974.

Summers, B. *Missouri Orchids.* 2d ed. Jefferson City: Missouri Department of Conservation, 1987.

Szczawinski, A.E. *The Orchids of British Columbia.* Victoria: British Columbia Provincial Museum, 1975.

Wallace, J.E. *The Orchids of Maine.* Orono: University of Maine at Orono, 1951.

Whiting, R.E., and P.M. Catling. *Orchids of Ontario.* Ottawa: CanaColl Foundation, 1986.

Williams, J.G., A.E. Williams, and N. Arlott. *A Field Guide to Orchids of North America.* New York: Universe Books, 1983.

Williams, L.O. "The Orchidaceae of the Rocky Mountains." *American Midland Naturalist* 18, no. 5 (May 1937): 830–41.

Winterringer, G.S. *Wild Orchids of Illinois.* Springfield: Illinois State Museum, 1967.

Photo Credits

All photographs were taken by Paul Martin Brown except for the following, which were generously loaned by those credited. Several were taken at his behest for this project.

Jim Ackerman
  Cranichis muscosa
  Cyclopogon elatus
  Pelexia adnata
Heinz Baum
  Amerorchis rotundifolia forma *beckettiae*
Stanley A. Bentley
  Corallorhiza bentleyi
Ronald A. Coleman
  Corallorhiza maculata var. *mexicana*
  Hexalectris revoluta
  Piperia colemanii
  Piperia cooperi
  Piperia elegans subsp. *decurtata*
  Piperia leptopetala
  Piperia michaelii
  Piperia yadonii
  Schiedeella arizonica
Frank Craighead
  Govenia floridana
Shirley Curtis
  Amerorchis rotundifolia forma *lineata*
Kerry Dressler
  Maxillaria parviflora
Bent Fredskild
  Platanthera hyperborea

Roger Hammer
  Basiphyllaea corallicola
  Prescottia oligantha
Hal Horwitz
  Platanthera chapmanii
Mark Larocque
  Malaxis wendtii
Joe Liggio
  Dichromanthus cinnabarinus
  Hexalectris grandiflora
  Hexalectris nitida
Carlyle A. Luer
  Bulbophyllum pachyrachis
  Deiregyne confusa
  Epidendrum acunae
  Platanthera tipuloides var. *behringiana*
  Triphora amazonica
  Triphora craigheadii
Chuck M. McCartney
  Ponthieva brittoniae
  Vanilla dilloniana
Dennis Maleug
  Platanthera brevifolia
Cliff Pelchat
  Vanilla phaeantha
Dietrich and Ursula Rueckbrodt
  Platanthera obtusata subsp. *oligantha*
Chuck Sheviak
  Platanthera purpurascens
  Spiranthes infernalis
Miguel Soto Arenas
  Bletia purpurea forma *alba*

Index

Primary entries for taxa are in bold.

Acuña's star orchid 35
Adam-and-Eve 2
  yellow-flowered form 2
Adder's-mouth, Bayard's 61
  bog 63
  clustered 62
  fir-dwelling 60
  Florida 64
  green 65
    two-leaved form 65
    variegated-leaf form 65
  purple 63
  rat-tailed 64
  two-leaved 62
  Wendt's 65
  white 61
    two-leaved form 61
Alaskan hybrid spotted lady's-slipper 28
Alaskan Piperia 74
Amerorchis 161
  rotundifolia 2
    forma *angustifolia* 2
    forma *beckettiae* 2
    forma *immaculata* 2
    forma *lineata* 2
Ames' ladies'-tresses 104
Amesia gigantea 40
Anacheilum cochleatum var. *triandrum* 99
Andrews' hybrid fringed orchis 94
  lady's-slipper 28
Aplectrum 160
  hyemale 2
    forma *pallidum* 2
Arethusa 160
  bulbosa 3
    forma *albiflora* 3, 130

    forma *subcaerulea* 3, 130
Arizona crested coralroot 50
Ash Meadows ladies'-tresses 108
Auricled twayblade 55
  three-leaved form 55
Autumn coralroot 17
  yellow-stemmed form 17
  Pringle's 17

Basiphyllaea **160**
  angustifolia 3
  corallicola 3
Bayard's adder's-mouth 61
Beadlea cranichoides 21
  elata 21
Beaked orchid 101
  Fakahatchee 102
    golden-yellow-flowered form 102
  leafless 102
    golden-bronze-flowered form (Folsom's) 101
    white/green-flowered form 101
  hoary 102
Bearded grass-pink 7
Behring orchid 93
Beloglottis **163**
  costaricensis 4, 188, 189
Bentley's coralroot 14
Bicolor hybrid fringed orchis 94
Big Bend National Park, Texas 33, 65
Blephariglottis
  blephariglottis 75
  chapmanii 77
  conspicua 76
  grandiflora 82
  peramoena 90
  psycodes 91

Bletia 164
   florida **4**, 164, 190
   patula **5**, 164
   purpurea **5**, 164
     forma *alba* **5**, 131
Bletilla 164
   striata **6**, 190
Blunt-leaved rein orchis 88
   dwarfed form 88
   multiple-leaved form 88
   few-flowered 88
Bog adder's-mouth 63
   candles 81
   orchid, cloistered 93
     Thurber's 86
     green 83
     northern 84
   orchis, short-spurred 92
Brassavola cordata 185
Brassia 158
   caudata **6**
Broad-leaved helleborine 40
   albino form 40
   green-flowered form 40
   variegated form 40
   white-flowered form 40
   yellow-flowered form 40
Broad-lipped twayblade 57
   three-leaved form 57
Bronze green-fly orchis 37
Bulbophyllum 158
   pachyrhachis **7**
Butterfly orchid, dwarf 100
   false 66
   Florida 34
     white-lipped form 34
   rufous 34

California lady's-slipper 22
×*Caloarethusa* 185
Calopogon 163, 164
   barbatus **7**
     var. *multiflorus* **8**
   multiflorus **8**, 165
   oklahomensis **8**, 165, 195
   pallidus **9**, 165
     forma *albiflorus* **9**

   pulchellus **9**
     var. *latifolius* **9**
     var. *simpsonii* **10**
   tuberosus
     var. *latifolius* **9**, 191
     var. *nanus* 191
     var. *simpsonii* **10**, 165
       forma *niveus* **10**, 187
     var. *tuberosus* **9**, 165
       forma *albiflorus* **9**
Calypso 159, 165
   bulbosa subsp. *occidentalis* **11**
     var. *americana* **10**, 165
       forma *albiflora* **10**, 132
       forma *rosea* **10**, 132
     var. *occidentalis* **11**, 165
       forma *nivea* **11**
Campylocentrum 157
   filiforme 48
   pachyrrhizum **11**
   porrectum 48
Canby's hybrid fringed orchis 94
Canelo Hills ladies'-tresses 106
Carteria corallicola 3
Carter's orchid 3
Case's ladies'-tresses 105
   Nova Scotian ladies'-tresses 105
Cattleya spp. 185
Centrogenium setaceum 187, 189
Cephalanthera 159, 192
   austiniae **12**, 192
Chamisso's orchid 77
Channell's hybrid fringed orchis 94
Chapman's fringed orchis 94
Chatterbox 40
Checkered rattlesnake orchis 44
Cigar orchid 29
Cinnabar ladies'-tresses 33
Clamshell orchid, Florida 99
   pale-flowered form 99
Cleistes 163, 165
   bifaria **12**, 165, 194
   divaricata **13**, 165
     forma *leucantha* **13**, 133, 194
     var. *bifaria* **12**, 194
Climbing epidendrum 38
Cloistered bog orchid 93

Clustered adder's-mouth 62
　lady's-slipper 23
Coeloglossum 161, 165
　bracteatum 14
　viride
　　subsp. *bracteatum* 14
　　var. *islandicum* 13
　　var. *virescens* 14, 165
　　var. *viride* 13, 165
Coleman's piperia 70
Columbia hybrid lady's-slipper 28
Commercial vanilla 127
Common grass-pink 9
　white-flowered form 9
　twayblade 59
Cone-bearing epidendrum 39
Cooper's stout-spire orchid 70
Copper ladies'-tresses 67
Corallorhiza 159, 166
　arizonica 50
　bentleyi 14, 166, 196
　bigelovii 18
　corallorhiza 19
　maculata
　　subsp. *mertensiana* 16
　　subsp. *occidentalis* 16
　　var. *maculata* 15, 166
　　　forma *flavida* 15, 133
　　　forma *rubra* 15
　　var. *mexicana* 15, 166, 195
　　var. *occidentalis* 16, 166, 195
　　　forma *aurea* 16
　　　forma *immaculata* 16, 134, 195
　　　forma *intermedia* 16
　　　forma *punicea* 16
　mertensiana 16, 166
　　forma *albolabia* 16, 134
　　forma *pallida* 16
　mexicana 15
　micrantha 17
　multiflora 15
　odontorhiza
　　var. *odontorhiza* 17, 167
　　　forma *flavida* 17
　　var. *pringlei* 17, 167, 195
　pringlei 17
　purpurea 16

striata
　forma *fulva* 18
　var. *striata* 18, 166
　　forma *eburnea* 18, 135
　var. *vreelandii* 18, 166
　　forma *flavida* 18
trifida 19, 166
　var. *verna* 19
wisteriana 19, 166
　forma *albolabia* 19
　forma *rubra* 19, 135
Coralroot
　Arizona crested 50
　autumn 17
　　yellow-stemmed form 17
　　Pringle's 17
　Bentley's 14
　crested 50
　　white-lipped form 50
　early 19
　Greenman's crested 48
　Mexican spotted 15
　Pringle's autumn 17
　recurved crested 49
　shining crested 49
　spotted 16
　　red-stemmed form 16
　　yellow-stemmed 16
　striped 18
　　yellow/white form 18
　Vreeland's 18
　　yellow/white form 18
　western 16
　　pale colored form 16
　　white-flowered form 16
　western spotted 15
　　brown-stemmed form 15
　　golden yellow/spotted form 15
　　red-stemmed form 15
　　yellow spotless form 15
　Wister's 19
　　red-stemmed form 19
　　white-flowered form 19
Correll's hybrid rein orchis 94
Costa Rican ladies'-tresses 4
Cowhorn orchid 29
　yellow 29

Craighead's noddingcaps 122
Crane-fly orchis 119
   green-leaved form 119
Cranichis 162
   muscosa 20
Crested coralroot 50
      white-lipped form 50
   Arizona 50
   orchis, orange 79
      pale-flowered form 79
Crestless plume orchid 101
   yellow-flowered form 101
Crimson lepanthopsis 53
Criosanthes arietina 22
Crooked-spur orchid 11
Cuban ground orchid 95
Cyclopogon 163, 167
   cranichoides 20, 167, 188, 189, 192
      forma *albolabius* 20
   elatus 21, 167, 188, 189, 192
Cypripedium 159, 167
   acaule 21, 167
      forma *albiflorum* 21, 136
      forma *biflorum* 21
   album 191
   arietinum 22, 168
      forma *albiflorum* 22
      forma *biflorum* 22, 136
   calceolus
      var. *parviflorum* 25, 26
      var. *planipetalum* 26, 191
      var. *pubescens* 25, 187, 191, 193
   californicum 22, 168
   candidum 23, 167
   daultonii 24
   fasciculatum 23, 167
   flavescens 25
   guttatum 24, 67, 191, 192
      subsp. *yatabeanum* 28
      var. *yatabeanum* 28
   kentuckiense 24, 168, 195
      forma *pricei* 24
   knightiae 23
   montanum 25, 168
      forma *praetertinctum* 25
      forma *welchii* 25
   parviflorum

      var. *makasin* 26, 168, 191
      var. *parviflorum* 25, 168, 195
         forma *albolabium* 25
      var. *planipetalum* 26
      var. *pubescens* 26, 168, 187, 191, 193
   passerinum 27, 168
      var. *minganense* 27
   pubescens 26
      var. *makasin* 26
   reginae 27, 167
      forma *albolabium* 27, 137
   spectabile 27
   veganum 26
   yatabeanum 28, 167, 191, 192
   ×*alaskanum* 28, 137, 196
   ×*andrewsii* nm *andrewsii* 28, 138, 191
   ×*andrewsii* nm *favillianum* 28
   ×*andrewsii* nm *landonii* 28
   ×*columbianum* 28, 196
   ×*favillianum* 28, 191
   ×*landonii* 28, 191
Cyrtopodium 158, 169
   andersonii 29, 189
   glutiniferum 29
   paranaense 29
   polyphyllum 29, 169, 189
   punctatum 29, 169
Cytherea bulbosa 10

Dactylorhiza 164
   aristata
      var. *aristata* 30, 169
         forma *alba* 30
      var. *kodiakensis* 30, 169
         forma *perbracteata* 30, 169
         forma *rosea* 30
   cf. *fuchsii* 31
   comosa subsp. *majalis* 31
   maculata 31, 191, 193
   majalis 31
      subsp. *praetermissa* 31, 169, 195
         forma *albiflora* 31, 139
      var. *junialis* 31, 169, 191, 193
      var. *praetermissa* 31
   praetermissa var. *junialis* 31
   viridis 13
Deiregyne 160

confusa **32**, 192, 193
    durangensis 32
Delicate ionopsis 51
Dendrophylax 157, 187, 190, 191
    lindenii **32**, 191
Densely-flowered maxillaria 66
Dichromanthus 162
    cinnabarinus **33**, 192, 193
    michuacanus 118
Dillon's vanilla 125
Dingy-flowered star orchid 35
    red-leaved form 35
Downy rattlesnake orchis 43
Dragon's-mouth 3
    lilac-blue flowered form 3
    white-flowered form 3
Dwarf butterfly orchid 100

Early coralroot 19
Eastern fairy-slipper 10
    pink-flowered form 10
    white-flowered form 10
Eastern prairie fringed orchis 86
Eaton's ladies'-tresses 107
Eburophyton austinae 12
Elegant piperia 71
Eltroplectris 161, 187
    calcarata **33**, 189
Encyclia 158, 169, 187, 189
    bahamensis 34
    boothiana var. *erythronioides* 99
    cochleata
        subsp. *triandra* 99
        var. *triandra* 99
    hodgeana 185
    pygmaea 100
    rufa **34**, 169, 190
    tampensis **34**, 169
        forma *albolabia* **34**, 139
Epidendrum
    climbing 38
    cone-bearing 39
    night-fragrant 37
    rigid 38
Epidendrum 157, 169
    acunae **35**, 170
    amphistomum **35**, 170, 189

    forma *rubrifolium* **35**, 140
    anceps **35**, 189
    bahamense 34
    blancheanum 35
    boothianum 99
    cochleatum
        subsp. *triandrum* 99
        var. *triandrum* 99
    conopseum
        var. *conopseum* **36**, 189
        var. *mexicanum* 37
    difforme **36**, 189
    erythronioides 99
    floridense **36**, 170, 189
    magnoliae
        var. *magnoliae* **36**, 170, 189
        var. *mexicanum* **37**, 170
    nocturnum **37**, 170
    pygmaeum 100
    cf. *radicans* **38**, 169, 190
    rigidum **38**, 170
    rufum 34
    strobiliferum **39**, 170
    tampense 34
Epipactis 159, 170
    atrorubens **39**, 170, 195
    gigantea **40**, 170
        forma *citrina* **40**
        forma *rubrifolia* **40**
    helleborine **40**, 170
        forma *alba* **40**
        forma *luteola* **40**, 140
        forma *monotropoides* **40**
        forma *variegata* **40**
        forma *viridens* **40**
    latifolia 40
    rubiginosa 39
Erythrodes querceticola 95, 187, 189
    var. *sagreana* 95, 189
Estes hybrid rein orchis 94
Eulophia 161, 187
    alta **41**
        forma *pallida* **41**
        forma *pelchatii* **41**
    ecristata 101, 189
Eulophidium maculatum 67
Everglades National Park, Fla. 4, 6, 41, 68, 97

Fairy-slipper
  eastern 10
    pink-flowered form 10
    white-flowered form 10
  western 11
    white-flowered form 11
Fakahatchee beaked orchid 102
  golden yellow-flowered form 102
Fakahatchee Strand State Preserve, Fla. 7, 11, 35, 53, 66, 100, 102
False butterfly orchid 66
False water-spider orchid 45
Faville's hybrid yellow lady's-slipper 28
Fen orchis 55
Few-flowered blunt leaved rein orchis 88
Few-flowered rein-orchis 92
Fischer's orchid 30
  white-flowered form 30
Fissipes acaulis 21
Flat-spurred piperia 73
Florida adder's-mouth 64
Florida butterfly orchid 34
  white-lipped form 34
Florida clamshell orchid 99
  pale-colored form 99
Florida dollar orchid 99
Florida govenia 44
Florida ladies'-tresses 108
Florida oncidium 68
Florida star orchid 36
Florida's dancing lady 119
Folsom's hybrid ladies'-tresses 117
Fragrant ladies'-tresses 112
Fragrant orchid 45
Franklin's lady's-slipper 27
Fringed orchis
  Andrews' hybrid 94
  bicolor hybrid 94
  Canby's hybrid 94
  Channell's hybrid 94
  Chapman's 94
  eastern prairie 86
  green 85
  Holland River hybrid 94
  Keenan's hybrid 94
  large purple 82
    bicolor-flowered form 82

entire-lip form 82
  pink-flowered form 82
  white-flowered form 82
northern white 75
  entire-lip form 75
orange 78
pale 89
Reznicek's hybrid 94
small purple 91
  entire-lip form 91
  pink-flowered form 91
  spurless form 91
  white-flowered form 91
southern white 76
western prairie 90
Frog orchid 22
Frosted pleurothallis 96

Galeandra 159
  beyrichii 41, 189
  bicarinata **41**, 189, 190
Galearis 161
  spectabilis **42**
    forma *gordinierii* **42**
    forma *willeyi* **42**
Galeorchis spectabilis 42
Ghost orchid 32
Giant ladies'-tresses 115
  white-lipped form 115
Giant rattlesnake orchis 42
  reticulated-leaved form 42, 142
Glandular ladies'-tresses 68
Goldie's pad-leaved orchis 87
Goodyera 159, 170
  decipiens 42
  oblongifolia **42**, 171
    forma *reticulata* 42
  pubescens **43**, 171
  repens **43**, 171
    forma *ophioides* **43**
  tesselata **44**, 171
Govenia 164
  floridana **44**, 189, 190
  utriculata 189, 190
Grass-leaved ladies'-tresses 117
Grass-pink
  bearded 7

common 9
   white-flowered form 9
many-flowered 8
Oklahoma 8
pale 9
   white-flowered form 9
Simpson's 10
   white-flowered form 10
Great Plains ladies'-tresses 111
Green adder's-mouth 65
   two-leaved form 65
Green bog orchis 83
Green fringed orchis 85
Green-fly orchis 36
   bronze 37
Greenman's crested coralroot 48
Ground orchid
   Cuban 95
   low 95
Gymnadenia 161
   albida subsp. *straminea* 100
   conopsea 45
Gymnadeniopsis
   clavellata 78
      var. *ophioglossoides* 78
   integra 87
   nivea 87
Gyrostachys
   laciniata 110
   ochroleuca 112
   stricta 115

Habenaria
   long-horned 46
   toothed 46
      form 46
Habenaria 61, 171
   albida var. *straminea* 100
   behringiana 93
   blephariglottis
      blephariglottis 75
      var. *conspicua* 75
      var. *integrilabia* 75
   borealis
      var. *albiflora* 80
      var. *viridiflora* 92
   bracteata 14

brevifolia 76
chorisiana 77
ciliaris 78
clavellata
   var. *clavellata* 78
   var. *ophioglossoides* 79
conopsea 45
conspicua 76
correlliana 85
cristata 79
dilatata
   var. *albiflora* 80
   var. *dilatata* 80
   var. *leucostachys* 81
distans 45, 171
elegans 71
   var. *maritima* 193
fimbriata 82
flava 81
   var. *herbiola* 82
   var. *virescens* 82
floribunda 46
garberi 46
grandiflora 82
greenei 71
herbiola 82
hookeri 83
hyperborea 75, 84
   var. *huronensis* 83
   var. *purpurascens* 92
integra 87
lacera 85
   var. *terrae-novae* 94
leucophaea 86
leucostachys 81
limosa 86
macroceratitis 46, 171, 189
macrophylla 87
maritima 71
michaelii 73
nivea 87
nuttallii 47
obtusata 88
   var. *oligantha* 88
***odontopetala* 46**, 171
   forma *heatonii* 46
orbiculata 89

Habenaria—continued
    var. *menziesii* 89
   peramoena 90
   psycodes 91
    var. *grandiflora* 82
   quinqueseta 47, 171
    var. *macroceratitis* 189
   repens 47, 171
   saccata 92
   sparsiflora 92
    var. *brevifolia* 76
    var. *laxiflora* 92
   straminea 100
   strictissima var. *odontopetala* 46
   thurberi 86
   unalascensis 74
    subsp. *elata* 72
    var. *elata* 72
    var. *maritima* 71
   viridis 13
    var. *bracteata* 14
    var. *interjecta* 14
   zothecina 93
Habenella odontopetala 46
Haitian pine-pink 5
Hammarbya paludosa 63
Harrisella 157
   filiformis 48
   porrecta 48
Heart-leaved twayblade 58
   alternate-leaved form 58
   green-flowered form 58
   three-leaved form 58
   variegated-leaved form 58
Helleborine
   broad-leaved 40
    albino form 40
    green-flowered form 40
    variegated-leaved form 40
    white-flowered form 40
    yellow-flowered form 40
   red 39
Helleborine gigantea 40
Hexalectris 159, 171
   grandiflora 48, 172
   mexicana 48
   nitida 49, 171

   revoluta 49, 172
   spicata
    var. **arizonica** 50, 172, 195
    var. **spicata** 50, 172
     forma *albolabia* 50
   warnockii 51, 171
Hildago ladies'-tresses 32
Hoary leafless beaked orchid 102
Holland River hybrid fringed orchis 94
Hooded ladies'-tresses 115
Hooker's orchis 83
   dwarfed form 83
Hormidium pygmaeum 99
Hybrid fringed orchid
   Andrews' 94
   bicolor 94
   Canby's 94
   Channell's 94
   Holland River 94
   Keenan's 94
   Reznicek's 94
Hybrid ladies'-tresses
   Folsom's 117
   Ichetucknee Springs 118
   intermediate 118
   northern 117
   Simpson's 118
   southern 118
Hybrid lady's-slipper
   Alaskan 28
   Andrews' 28
   Columbia 28
   Faville's 28
   Landon's 28
Hybrid rein orchis
   Correll's 94
   Estes 94
   Lassen 94
   Voss' 94
Hybrid twayblade
   Jones' 55
   Veltman's 59

Ibidium
   beckii 109
   cernuum 106
   floridanum 108

gracile 109
laciniatum 110
longilabre 110
lucayanum 67
ovale 113
plantagineum 111
praecox 115
strictum 115
tortile 116
vernale 117
Ichetucknee Springs hybrid ladies'-tresses 118
Intermediate hybrid ladies'-tresses 118
Ionopsis 158
   utricularioides 51
Isotria 163, 172
   affinis 52
   medeoloides 52, 172
   verticillata 52, 172
Ivory-lipped lady's-slipper 24
   white-flowered form 24

Javanese orchid, purple 103
Jones' hybrid twayblade 55
Jug orchid 95

Keenan's hybrid fringed orchis 94
Kodiak orchid 30
   leafy, flowerless form 30
   pink-flowered form 30

Lace orchid 72
Lace-lipped ladies'-tresses 110
Ladies'-tresses
   Ames' 104
   Ash Meadows 108
   Canelo Hills 106
   Case's ladies'-tresses 105
      Nova Scotian 105
   cinnabar 33
   copper 67
   Costa Rican 4
   Eaton's 107
   Florida 108
   Folsom's hybrid 117
   fragrant 112
   giant 115
      white-lipped form 115

glandular 68
grass-leaved 117
Great Plains 111
Hildago 32
Hooded 115
hybrid
   Folsom's 117
   Ichetucknee Springs 118
   Intermediate 118
   northern 117
   Simpson's 118
   southern 118
Ichetucknee Springs hybrid 118
intermediate hybrid 118
lace-lipped 110
little 117
long-lipped 110
Michoacan 118
Navasota 114
nodding 106
northern hybrid 117
   oval 113
   slender 109
red-spot 103
scarlet 101
shining 111
short-lipped 104
Simpson's hybrid 118
southern hybrid 118
   oval 113
   slender 109
speckled 67
Texas 104
Ute 107
Western 114
woodland 116
yellow 112
Lady's-slipper
   Alaskan hybrid spotted 28
   Andrews' hybrid 28
   California 22
   clustered 23
   Columbia hybrid 28
   Faville's hybrid 28
   Franklin's 27
   ivory-lipped 24
      white-flowered form 24

Lady's-slipper—*continued*
  Landon's hybrid 28
  large yellow 26
  mountain 25
    crimson edge-lipped form 25
    white-petalled form 25
  northern small yellow 26
  pink 21
    two-flowered form 21
    white-flowered form 21
  ram's-head 21
    two-flowered form 21
    white-flowered form 21
  showy lady's-slipper 27
    white-flowered form 27
  small white 23
  southern small yellow 25
    white-lipped form 25
  sparrow's egg 27
  spotted 24
    Alaskan hybrid 28
    yellow 28
  yellow
    large 26
    northern small 26
    southern small 25
Laelia 158
  rubescens 53, 190
Landon's hybrid lady's-slipper 28
Large purple fringed orchis 82
  bicolor-flowered form 82
  entire-lip form 82
  pink-flowered form 82
  white-flowered form 82
Large whorled pogonia 52
  yellow lady's-slipper 52
Lassen hybrid rein orchis 94
Lawn orchid 128
Leafless beaked orchid 101
  golden bronze-flowered form (Folsom's) 101
  white/green-flowered form 101
Leafless harrisella 48
Leafless vanilla 125
Least noddingcaps 123
Leochilus labiatus 185
Leopard marsh orchid 32

Lepanthes harrisii 53
Lepanthopsis 157
  melanantha 53
Lesser rattlesnake orchis 43
  white-veined leaf form 43
Leucorchis albida subsp. *straminea* 100
Lily-leaved rein orchis 94
Lily-leaved twayblade 54
  green-flowered form 54
Limnorchis
  arizonica 86
  behringiana 93
  brevifolia 76
  chorisiana 77
  dilatata 80
  ensifolia 92
  hyperborea 75, 84
  laxiflora 92
  leucostachys 81
  media 83
  purpurascens 82
  sparsiflora 92
  stricta 92
Limodorum
  multiflorum 8
  pallidum 9
  parviflorum 7
  pinetorum 8
  simpsonii 10
  tuberosum 9
Liparis 157
  eggersii 162, 172
  elata 54, 172
  liliifolia 54, 172
    forma *viridiflora* 54
  loeselii 55, 172
  nervosa 54
  ×*jonesii* 55, 196
Listera 163, 172
  auriculata 55, 173
    forma *trifolia* 55
  australis 56, 172
    forma *scottii* 56, 142
    forma *trifolia* 56, 142
    forma *viridis* 56
  borealis 56, 173
    forma *trifolia* 56, 142

caurina 57
convallarioides 57, 173
    forma *trifolia* 57
cordata
    subsp. *nephrophylla* 58
    var. *cordata* 58, 172
        forma *disjuncta* 58
        forma *trifolia* 58
        forma *variegata* 58, 144
        forma *viridens* 58
    var. *nephrophylla* 58, 173
        forma *rubescens* 58
    nephrophylla 58
    ovata 59, 173
    reniformis 59
    smallii 59, 173
        forma *variegata* 59
    ×*veltmanii* 59, 144, 196
Little club-spur orchis 78
    white-flowered form 78
Little ladies'-tresses 117
Loesel's twayblade 55
Long bracted green orchis 14
Long-horned habenaria 189
Long-lipped ladies'-tresses 110
Long-spurred piperia 72
Lophiaris
    carthagenensis 120
    lurida 121
    maculata 121
Low ground orchid 95

Macradenia 158
    lutescens 60
Malaxis 162, 163, 173
    abieticola 60, 174, 194, 195
    bayardii 61, 174
    brachypoda 61, 174, 191, 194, 195
        forma *bifolia* 61
    corymbosa 62
    diphyllos 62, 174, 194, 195
    ehrenbergii 63, 194
    floridana 64
    macrostachya 64, 194, 195
    monophyllos
        var. *brachypoda* 61, 191, 194, 195
        var. *diphyllos* 62, 194, 195
        var. *monophyllos* 62

montana 64
paludosa 63, 174
porphyrea 63, 173, 194
soulei 64, 174, 194, 195
spicata 64, 174
tenuis 60, 174, 194, 195
unifolia 65, 174
        forma *bifolia* 65
        forma *variegata* 65
    var. *bayardii* 61
wendtii 65, 173
Many-flowered grass-pink 8
Many-flowered tropidia 124
Marsh orchid
    leopard 32
    southern 32
Maxillaria 158, 174
    conferta 66, 174, 190
    crassifolia 66, 174
    parviflora 66, 174
    purpurea 66
    sanguinea 185
    sessilis 66
Mesadenus 163
    lucayanus 67, 188, 189, 192
    polyanthus 67
Mexican spotted coralroot 15
Michael's Piperia 73
Michaux's orchid 47
Michoacan ladies'-tresses 118
Microstylis
    porphyrea 63
    unifolia 65
Moccasin flower 21
Monkey-face orchis 85
Moss-loving cranichis 20
Mountain lady's-slipper 25
    crimson edge-lipped form 25
    white-petalled form 25
Mrs. Britton's shadow-witch 97

Navasota ladies'-tresses 114
Neolehmannia difformis 36
Neottia
    spurred 33
    tall 21
Neottia
    auriculata 55

Neottia—*continued*
  australis 56
  borealis 56
  gracilis 109
  lacera 109
  nephrophylla 58
  smallii 59
Newfoundland orchis 101
Night-fragrant epidendrum 37
Nodding ladies'-tresses 106
Noddingcaps
  Craighead's 122
  least 123
  Rickett's 123
  wide-leaved 123
Northern bracted green orchis 13
Northern club-spur orchis 79
Northern green bog orchis 84
  albino form 84
Northern hybrid ladies'-tresses 117
Northern oval ladies'-tresses 113
Northern rein orchis 84
Northern slender ladies'-tresses 109
Northern small yellow lady's-slipper 26
Northern tubercled orchis 82
  yellow-flowered form 82
Northern twayblade 56
  three-leaved form 56
Northern white fringed orchis 75
  entire-lip form 75
Nova Scotian ladies'-tresses, Case's 105
Nun orchid 69

Oblong-leaved vanilla 126
Oeceoclades 161
  maculata **67**, 190
Oklahoma grass-pink 8
Oncidium 162, 188
  bahamense 119, 190
  carthagenense 120, 190
  ensatum 68
  ***floridanum* 68**
  luridum 121, 187, 190
  undulatum 121
  variegatum 119
    var. *bahamense* 119
Orange crested orchis 79
  pale yellow-flowered form 79

Orange fringed orchis 78
Orchis
  aristata 30
  rotundifolia 2
  spectabilis 42

Pad-leaved orchis 89
  dwarfed form 89
  three-leaved form 89
Pale-flowered polystachya 97
Pale fringed orchis 89
Pale grass-pink 9
  white-flowered form 9
Pale laelia 53
Palm polly 32
Pelexia 161
  ***adnata* 161**, 190
  setacea 68
Phaius 162
  grandifolia 69
  ***tankervilleae* 69**, 190
Phantom orchid 12
Physurus
  querceticola 95
  sagreanus 95
Pine-pink 5
  white-flowered form 5
  Haitian 5
  slender 4
Pink lady's-slipper 21
  two-flowered form 21
  white-flowered form 21
Piperia
  Alaskan 74
  Coleman's 70
  elegant 71
  flat-spurred 73
  long-spurred 72
  Michael's 73
  Point Reyes 71
  slender white 69
  Yadon's 74
Piperia 159, 174
  ***candida* 69**, 175, 195
  ***colemanii* 70**, 175, 195
  ***cooperi* 70**, 175, 195
  elegans
    subsp. ***decurtata* 71**, 175, 195

subsp. *elegans* 71, 175, 193
   var. *elata* 193
elongata 72, 175, 193
   var. *michaelii* 73
lancifolia 72
leptopetala 72, 175, 195
longispica 72
maritima 193
michaelii 73, 175
multiflora 71
transversa 73, 175, 195
unalascensis 74, 175
yadonii 74, 175, 195
Platanthera 160, 161, 162, 175
albida var. *straminea* 100, 192, 193, 194
aquilonis 75, 191, 192, 193, 194
   forma *alba* 75
blephariglottis
   var. *blephariglottis* 75, 175
      forma *holopetala* 75, 145
   var. *conspicua* 76, 175
brevifolia 76, 178, 193, 194
chapmanii 77, 175, 189, 193
chorisiana 77, 178
ciliaris 78, 175
clavellata
   var. *clavellata* 78, 177
      forma *slaughteri* 78
   var. *ophioglossoides* 79, 177
convallariaefolia 94, 179
cristata 79, 175
   forma *straminea* 79
dilatata
   var. *albiflora* 80, 178
   var. *dilatata* 80, 178
   var. *leucostachys* 81, 178
flava
   var. *flava* 81, 177
   var. *herbiola* 82, 177
      forma *lutea* 82
gracilis 115
grandiflora 82, 177
   forma *albiflora* 82, 177
   forma *bicolor* 82, 177
   forma *carnea* 82, 177
   forma *mentotonsa* 82, 177
hookeri 83, 178
   forma *abbreviata* 83, 146, 191, 194

   var. *abbreviata* 191, 194
huronensis 83, 179, 193, 194
hyperborea 84, 179, 191, 193
   var. *gracilis* 193, 194
   var. *huronensis* 83
   var. *hyperborea* 193, 194
   var. *purpurascens* 92, 193, 194
   var. *viridiflora* 92, 193, 194
integra 87, 176
integrilabia 85, 176
lacera 85, 176
   var. *terrae-novae* 94, 193
leucophaea 86, 177
leucostachys 81
limosa 86, 179
macrophylla 87, 178, 193–94
nivea 87, 177
obtusata
   subsp. *obtusata* 88, 178
      forma *collectanea* 88, 191, 194
      forma *foliosa* 88
   var. *collecteana* 194
   subsp. *oligantha* 88, 178
oligantha 88
orbiculata 89, 178, 193–94
      forma *trifolia* 89
      forma *lehorsii* 89, 191
   var. *lehorsii* 89
   var. *macrophylla* 191, 193, 194
pallida 89, 176, 195
parvula 88
peramoena 90, 176
praeclara 90, 177, 195
psycodes 91, 177
   forma *albiflora* 91
   forma *ecalcarata* 91
   forma *rosea* 91
   forma *varians* 91
purpurascens 92, 179, 193, 194
repens 47
saccata 92
sparsiflora
   var. *brevifolia* 193, 194
   var. *ensifolia* 92
   var. *sparsiflora* 92, 179
stricta 92, 179
tipuloides var. *behringiana* 93, 178
unalascensis 74

Platanthera—*continued*
    subsp. *elata* 72
    subsp. *maritima* 71
    var. *maritima* 71
   zothecina **93**, 178, 195
   ×*andrewsii* **94**, 146, 193
   ×*bicolor* **94**, 147
   ×*canbyi* **94**, 189
   ×*channellii* **94**, 147, 189, 190, 196
   ×*chapmanii* 77, 189, 193
   ×*correllii* **94**, 196
   ×*estesii* **94**, 196
   ×*hollandiae* **94**, 196
   ×*keenanii* **94**, 196
   ×*lassenii* **94**, 196
   ×*media* 83, 193, 194
   ×*reznicekii* **94**, 196
   ×*vossii* **94**, 196
Platypus altus 41
Platythelys 161, 187
   querceticola **95**, 179, 189
   sagreana **95**, 179, 189, 190
Pleurothallis 157
   gelida **96**
Plume orchid, crestless 101
   yellow-flowered form 101
Pogonia 163
   affinis 52
   bifaria 12
   divaricata 13
   ophioglossoides **96**
     forma *albiflora* **96**, 148
     forma *brachypogon* **96**, 148
   pendula 124
   verticillata 52
Point Reyes piperia 71
Polyradicion lindenii 32
Polyrrhiza lindenii 32, 187, 190, 191
Polystachya 158
   concreta **97**, 189
   flavescens 97, 189
   luteola 97
   minuta 97
Ponthieva 160, 163
   brittoniae **97**, 179
   racemosa **98**, 179
     var. *brittonae* 97

Prescottia 163
   oligantha **98**
Pringle's autumn coralroot 17
Prosthechea 158, 187, 189
   boothiana
     subsp. *erythronioides* 99
     var. *erythronioides* **99**, 180
   cochleata
     subsp. *triandra* 99
     var. *triandra* **99**, 180
       forma *albidoflava* **99**, 149, 189
   pygmaea **100**, **180**
Pseudodiphryllum chorisianum 77
Pseudorchis 161
   albida subsp. *straminea* 100, 193, 194
   albida var. *straminea* 193
   straminea **100**, 193
Pteroglossaspis 163, 187
   ecristata **101**, 189
     forma *flava* **101**
Purple adder's-mouth 63
Purple fringed orchis
   large 82
   small 91
Purple fringeless orchis 90
Purple Javanese orchid 103
Putty-root 2
   yellow-flowered form 2

Ragged orchis 85
Ram's-head lady's-slipper 22
   two-flowered form 22
   white-flowered form 22
Rat-tail orchid 7
Rat-tailed adder's-mouth 64
Rattlesnake orchis
   checkered 44
   downy 43
   dwarf 43
   giant 42
   Menzies' 42
Recurved crested coralroot 49
Red helleborine 39
Red-spot ladies'-tresses 103
Rein orchis
   blunt-leaved 88
     dwarfed form 88

multiple-leaved form 88
Correll's hybrid 94
Estes hybrid 94
few-flowered blunt-leaved 88
Lassen hybrid 94
lily-leaved 94
northern 84
short-leaved 76
Voss' hybrid 94
Restrepiella ophiocephala 185, 189
Reznicek's hybrid fringed orchid 94
Rickett's noddingcaps 123
Rigid epidendrum 38
Rose pogonia 96
short-bearded form 96
white-flowered form 96
Rufous butterfly orchid 34

Sacoila 159, 161, 180
lanceolata
var. *lanceolata* 101, 180, 188, 189, 192
forma *albidaviridis* 101, 150, 188, 189, 192
forma *folsomii* 101, 150
var. *paludicola* 102, 180, 188, 189, 192
forma *aurea* 102, 151
var. squamulosa 102
squamulosa 102, 180, 190
Scentless vanilla 126
Schiedeella 160
arizonica 103, 192, 194
confusa 32
fauci-sanguinea 103
parasitica 103
Scott's southern twayblade 56
Shadow-witch 98
Mrs. Britton's 97
Shining crested coralroot 49
Shining ladies'-tresses 111
Short-leaved rein orchis 76
Short-lipped ladies'-tresses 104
Short-spurred bog orchis 91
Showy lady's-slipper 27
white-flowered form 27
Showy orchis 42
pink-flowered form 42
white-flowered form 42

Sierra rein-orchid 81
Simpson's grass-pink 10
white-flowered form 10
Simpson's hybrid ladies'-tresses 118
Slender bog orchis 92
Slender pine-pink 4
Slender white piperia 69
Small prescottia 98
Small purple fringed orchis 91
entire-lip form 91
pink-flowered form 91
spurless form 91
white-flowered form 91
Small round-leaved orchis 2
lined-lip form 2
narrow-leaved form 2
white-flowered form 2
white-lipped form 2
Small's twayblade 59
variegated-leaved form 59
Small white lady's-slipper 23
Small whorled pogonia 52
Small yellow lady's-slipper
northern 26
southern 25
Snowy orchis 87
Southern hybrid ladies'-tresses 118
Southern ladies'-tresses 116
Southern marsh orchid 31
white-flowered form 32
Southern oval ladies'-tresses 113
Southern slender ladies'-tresses 109
Southern small yellow lady's-slipper 25
white-lipped form 25
Southern tubercled orchis 81
Southern twayblade 56
many-leaved form (Scott's) 56
green-flowered form 56
three-leaved form 56
Southern vanilla 127
Southern white fringed orchis 76
Sparrow's egg lady's-slipper 27
Spathoglottis 162, 164
plicata 103, 190
Speckled ladies'-tresses 20
white-lipped form 20
Spider orchid 6

Spiranthes 160, 162, 180
  adnata 68
  amesiana 104, 181, 183, 190
  beckii 109
  brevilabris 104, 182, 188, 192
    var. *floridana* 192
  calcarata 33
  casei
    var. *casei* 105, 192, 195
    var. *novaescotiae* 105, 195
  cernua 106, 188
    var. *ochroleuca* 112
    var. *odorata* 188
  cinnabarina 33, 192, 193
  confusa 32
  costaricensis 4, 188, 189, 192
  cranichoides 20, 188, 189, 192
  delitescens 106, 181, 192, 195
  diluvialis 107, 182, 195
  durangensis 32, 192, 193
  eatonii 107, 182, 190, 195
  elata 21, 188, 189, 192
  fauci-sanguinea 103
  floridana 108, 182, 192
  gracilis 188
    var. *brevilabris* 104
    var. *floridana* 108
  graminea 106, 192
  grayi 117, 188
  infernalis 108, 182, 195
  intermedia 105, 192
  lacera
    var. *gracilis* 109, 183, 188
    var. *lacera* 109, 183
  laciniata 110, 181
  lanceolata
    var. *lanceolata* 188, 189, 192
    var. *luteoalba* 188, 189, 192
    var. *paludicola* 188, 189, 192
  longilabris 110, 183
  lucayana 67, 192
  lucida 111, 181
  magnicamporum 111, 183
  michuacana 118, 192, 193
  ochroleuca 112, 188
  odorata 112, 188
  orchioides 101
  ovalis
    var. *erostellata* 113, 182, 190, 195
    var. *ovalis* 113, 182
  parasitica 103, 192, 194
  parksii 114, 183
  plantaginea 111
  polyanthus 67, 188, 189, 192
  porrifolia 114, 181
  praecox 115, 181
    forma *albolabia* 115, 151
  romanzoffiana 115, 181
    var. *diluvialis* 107
    var. *porrifolia* 114
  simplex 117
  sinensis 185
  squamulosa 102
  stricta 115
  sylvatica 116, 181, 190, 195
  torta 116, 181, 183, 188, 192
  tortilis 116, 188, 192
  tuberosa 117, 183, 188
    var. *grayi* 117
  unalascensis 74
  vernalis 117, 181
  ×*australis* 118
  ×**borealis** 117, 152, 196
  ×**folsomii** 117, 152, 190, 196
  ×**intermedia** 118, 196
  ×**itchetuckneensis** 118, 190, 196
  ×**meridionalis** 118, 153, 190, 196
  ×**simpsonii** 118, 196
  ×*steigeri* 192
Spotted African orchis 67
Spotted coralroot 15
  red-stemmed form 15
  yellow-stemmed form 15
  Mexican 15
  western 16
    brown-stemmed form 16
    golden yellow/spotted form 16
    red-stemmed form 16
    yellow spotless form 16
Spotted lady's-slipper 24
  Alaskan hybrid 28
Spotted mule-eared orchid 121
  unspotted with a yellow-green base 121
Spread-eagle orchid 120
Spreading pogonia 13
  white-flowered form 13
  upland 13
Spurred neottia 33

Star orchid
  Acuña's 35
  dingy-flowered 35
    red-leaved form 35
  Florida 36
Stelis gelida 96
Stenorrhynchos 160
  cinnabarina 33
  lanceolatum 101
  michuacanum **118**, 192, 193
  orchioides 101
  squamulosum 102
Stenorrhynchus calcaratus 33
Stout-spire orchid, Coopers 70
Stream orchid 40
  red-leaved form 40
  yellow-flowered form 40
Striped coralroot 18
  yellow/white form 18
  Vreeland's 18
    yellow/white form 18

Tall neottia 2
Tall twayblade 54
Tall white northern bog orchis 80
Tetramicra cf. *caniculata* 185, 189
Texas ladies'-tresses 104
Texas purple-spike 48
Thin-leaved vanilla 126
Three birds orchid 124
  blue-flowered form 124, 153
  multi-colored form 124
  white-flowered form 124
Thurber's bog orchid 86
Tipularia 159
  discolor **119**
    forma *viridifolia* **119**
  unifolia 119
Tolumnia 158, 188
  bahamensis **119**, 190
  variegata 119
Toothed habenaria 46
  albino form 46
Trichocentrum 158, 183, 188
  carthagenense **120**, **183**, 190
  maculatum 121
  *undulatum_***121**, 183, 187, 190
    forma *flavovirens* 121
Trinidad macradenia 60

Triphora 164, 184
  amazonica **122**, 184, 188, 194
  craigheadii **122**, 184
  cubensis 123
  gentianoides **123**, 184
  latifolia 122, 188, 194
  pendula 124
  rickettii **123**, 184
  trianthophora
    subsp. *mexicana* 185
    subsp. *trianthophora* 124, 184
      forma *albidoflava* 124
      forma *caerulea* 124, 153
      forma *rossii* 124
  yucatanensis 123
Tropidia 164
  polystachya **124**
Twayblade
  auricled 55
    three-leaved form 55
  broad-lipped 57
    three-leaved form 57
  common 59
  heart-leaved 58
    alternate-leaved form 58
    green-flowered form 58
    three-leaved form 58
    variegated-leaved form 58
  Jones' hybrid 55
  lily-leaved 54
    green-flowered form 54
  Loesel's 55
  northern 56
    three-leaved form 56
  Scott's southern 56
  Small's 59
  Southern 56
    many-leaved form (Scott's) 56
    green-flowered form 56
    three-leaved form 56
  tall 54
  Veltman's hybrid 59
  western heart-leaved 58
    reddish-flowered form 58
Two-keeled galeandra 41
Two-leaved adder's-mouth 62

Upland spreading pogonia 12
Urn orchid 6

Ute ladies'-tresses 107

Vanilla
    commercial 127
    Dillon's 125
    leafless 125
    oblong-leaved 126
    scentless 126
    southern 127
    thin-leaved 126
Vanilla 157, 184
    articulata 125
    barbellata **125**, 184
    dilloniana **125**, 184
    eggersii 125
    fragrans 127
    inodora 126, 184, 188
    mexicana **126**, 188
    phaeantha **126**, 184
    planifolia **127**, 184
    pompona **127**, 184
Veltman's hybrid twayblade 59
Voss' hybrid rein orchis 94
Vreeland's striped coralroot 18
    yellow/white form 18

Water spider orchid 47
    false 45
Wendt's adder's-mouth 65
Western coralroot 16
    pale-colored form 16
    white-flowered form 16
Western fairy-slipper 11
    white-flowered form 11

Western heart-leaved twayblade 58
    reddish-flowered form 58
Western ladies'-tresses 114
Western spotted coralroot 16
    brown-stemmed form 16
    golden yellow/spotted form 16
    red-stemmed form 16
    yellow spotless form 16
White adder's-mouth 61
    two-leaved form 61
Whorled pogonia
    large 52
    small 52
Wide-leaved noddingcaps 122
Wild coco 41
    pale colored form 41
    white and green-flowered form 41
Wister's coralroot 19
    red-stemmed form 19
    white-flowered form 19
Woodland ladies'-tresses 116
Worm-vine 125

Yadon's Piperia 74
Yellow cowhorn orchid 29
Yellow fringeless orchis 84
Yellow ladies'-tresses 112
Yellow lady's-slipper 25, 26
    large 26
    northern small 26
    southern small 25

Zeuxine 164
    strateumatica **128**

Personal Checklist

This checklist is provided for those who wish to keep a record of what they have seen, when, and where.

Amerorchis rotundifolia
small round-leaved orchis
    forma *angustifolia*
    forma *beckettiae*
    forma *immaculata*
    forma *lineata*

Aplectrum hyemale
putty-root, Adam-and-Eve
    forma *pallidum*

Arethusa bulbosa
dragon's-mouth
    forma *albiflora*
    forma *subcaerulea*

Basiphyllaea corallicola
Carter's orchid

Beloglottis costaricensis
Costa Rican ladies'-tresses

*Bletia florida**
slender pine-pink

*Bletia patula**
Haitian pine-pink

Bletia purpurea
pine-pink
    forma *alba*

*Bletilla striata**
urn orchid

Brassia caudata
spider orchid

Bulbophyllum pachyrachis
rat-tail orchid

Calopogon barbatus
bearded grass-pink

Calopogon multiflorus
many-flowered grass-pink

Calopogon oklahomensis
Oklahoma grass-pink

Calopogon pallidus
pale grass-pink
    forma *albiflorus*

Calopogon tuberosus var. *tuberosus*
common grass-pink
   forma *albiflorus*
Calopogon tuberosus var. *simpsonii*
Simpson's grass-pink
   forma *niveus*

Calypso bulbosa var. *americana*
eastern fairy-slipper
   forma *albiflora*
   forma *rosea*
Calypso bulbosa var. *occidentalis*
western fairy-slipper
   forma *nivea*

Campylocentrum pachyrrhizum
crooked-spur orchid

Cephalanthera austiniae
phantom orchid

Cleistes bifaria
upland spreading pogonia

Cleistes divaricata
spreading pogonia
   forma *leucantha*

Coeloglossum viride var. *viride*
northern bracted green orchis
Coeloglossum viride var. *virescens*
long-bracted green orchis

Corallorhiza bentleyi
Bentley's coralroot

Corallorhiza maculata var. *maculata*
spotted coralroot
   forma *flavida*
   forma *rubra*

Corallorhiza maculata var. *mexicana*
Mexican spotted coralroot
Corallorhiza maculata var. *occidentalis*
western spotted coralroot
   forma *aurea*
   forma *immaculata*
   forma *intermedia*
   forma *punicea*

Corallorhiza mertensiana
western coralroot
   forma *albolabia*
   forma *pallida*

Corallorhiza odontorhiza var.
   odontorhiza
autumn coralroot
   forma *flavida*
Corallorhiza odontorhiza var. *pringlei*
Pringle's autumn coralroot

Corallorhiza striata var. *striata*
striped coralroot
   forma *eburnea*
Corallorhiza striata var. *vreelandii*
Vreeland's striped coralroot
   forma *flavida*

Corallorhiza trifida
early coralroot

Corallorhiza wisteriana
Wister's coralroot
   forma *albolabia*
   forma *rubra*

Cranichis muscosa
moss-loving cranichis

Cyclopogon cranichoides
speckled ladies'-tresses
 forma *albolabius*

Cyclopogon elatus
tall neottia

Cypripedium acaule
pink lady's-slipper, moccasin flower
 forma *albiflorum*
 forma *biflorum*

Cypripedium arietinum
ram's-head lady's-slipper
 forma *albiflorum*
 forma *biflorum*

Cypripedium californicum
California lady's-slipper

Cypripedium candidum
small white lady's-slipper

Cypripedium fasciculatum
clustered lady's-slipper

Cypripedium guttatum
spotted lady's-slipper

Cypripedium kentuckiense
ivory-lipped lady's-slipper
 forma *pricei*

Cypripedium montanum
mountain lady's-slipper
 forma *praetertinctum*
 forma *welchii*

Cypripedium parviflorum var.
 parviflorum
southern small yellow lady's-slipper
 forma *albolabium*
Cypripedium parviflorum var. *makasin*
northern small yellow lady's-slipper
Cypripedium parviflorum var. *pubescens*
large yellow lady's-slipper

Cypripedium passerinum
sparrow's egg lady's-slipper, Franklin's
 lady's-slipper

Cypripedium reginae
showy lady's-slipper
 forma *albolabium*

Cypripedium yatabeanum
yellow spotted lady's-slipper

Hybrids:
Cypripedium ×*alaskanum*
Alaskan hybrid spotted lady's-slipper
Cypripedium ×*andrewsii* nm *andrewsii*
Andrews' hybrid lady's-slipper
Cypripedium ×*andrewsii* nm
 favillianum
Faville's hybrid lady's-slipper
Cypripedium ×*andrewsii* nm *landonii*
Landon's hybrid lady's-slipper
Cypripedium ×*columbianum*
Columbia hybrid lady's-slipper

*Cyrtopodium polyphyllum**
yellow cowhorn orchid

Cyrtopodium punctatum
cowhorn orchid, cigar orchid

Dactylorhiza aristata var. *aristata*
Fischer's orchid
  forma *alba*
Dactylorhiza aristata var. *kodiakensis*
Kodiak orchid
  forma *rosea*
  forma *perbracteata*

Dactylorhiza majalis var. *junialis*
leopard marsh orchid
Dactylorhiza majalis subsp. *praetermissa*
southern marsh orchid
  forma *albiflora*

Deiregyne confusa
Hildago ladies'-tresses

Dendrophylax lindenii
ghost orchid, frog orchid, palm polly

Dichromanthus cinnabarinus
cinnabar ladies'-tresses

Eltroplectris calcarata
spurred neottia

Encyclia rufa
rufous butterfly orchid

Encyclia tampensis
Florida butterfly orchid
  forma *albolabia*

Epidendrum acunae
Acuña's star orchid

Epidendrum amphistomum
dingy-flowered star orchid
  forma *rubrifolium*

Epidendrum floridense
Florida star orchid

Epidendrum magnoliae var. *magnoliae*
green-fly orchis
Epidendrum magnoliae var. *mexicanum*
bronze green-fly orchis

Epidendrum nocturnum
night-fragrant epidendrum

Epidendrum cf. *radicans*
climbing epidendrum

Epidendrum rigidum
rigid epidendrum

Epidendrum strobiliferum
cone-bearing epidendrum

*Epipactis atrorubens**
red helleborine

Epipactis gigantea
stream orchid
  forma *citrina*
  forma *rubrifolia*

Epipactis helleborine
broad-leaved helleborine
  forma *alba*
  forma *luteola*
  forma *monotropoides*
  forma *variegata*
  forma *viridens*

Eulophia alta
wild coco
  forma *pallida*
  forma *pelchatii*

Galeandra bicarinata
two keeled galeandra

Galearis spectabilis
showy orchis
   forma *gordinierii*
   forma *willeyi*

Goodyera oblongifolia
giant rattlesnake orchis
   forma *reticulata*

Goodyera pubescens
downy rattlesnake orchis

Goodyera repens
lesser rattlesnake orchis
   forma *ophioides*

Goodyera tesselata
checkered rattlesnake orchis

Govenia floridana
Florida govenia

*Gymnadenia conopsea**
fragrant orchid

Habenaria distans
false water-spider orchid

Habenaria macroceratitis
long-horned habenaria

Habenaria odontopetala
toothed habenaria
   forma *heatonii*

Habenaria quinqueseta
Michaux's orchid

Habenaria repens
water spider orchid

Harrisella porrecta
leafless harrisella

Hexalectris grandiflora
Greenman's crested coralroot

Hexalectris nitida
shining crested coralroot

Hexalectris revoluta
recurved crested coralroot

Hexalectris spicata var. *spicata*
crested coralroot
   forma *albolabia*
Hexalectris spicata var. *arizonica*
Arizona crested coralroot

Hexalectris warnockii
Texas purple-spike

Ionopsis utricularioides
delicate ionopsis

Isotria medeoloides
small whorled pogonia

Isotria verticillata
large whorled pogonia

*Laelia rubescens**
pale laelia

Lepanthopsis melanantha
crimson lepanthopsis

Liparis elata
tall twayblade

Liparis liliifolia
lily-leaved twayblade
forma *viridiflora*

Liparis loeselii
Loesel's twayblade, fen orchis

Hybrid:
Liparis ×*jonesii*
Jones' hybrid twayblade

Listera auriculata
auricled twayblade
forma *trifolia*

Listera australis
southern twayblade
forma *scottii*
forma *trifolia*
forma *viridis*

Listera borealis
northern twayblade
forma *trifolia*

Listera caurina
northwestern twayblade

Listera convallarioides
broad-lipped twayblade
forma *trifolia*

Listera cordata var. *cordata*
heart-leaved twayblade
forma *disjuncta*
forma *trifolia*
forma *variegata*
forma *viridens*
Listera cordata var. *nephrophylla*
western heart-leaved twayblade
forma *rubescens*

*Listera ovata**
common twayblade

Listera smallii
Small's twayblade
forma *variegata*

Hybrid:
Listera ×*veltmanii*
Veltman's twayblade

Macradenia lutescens
Trinidad macradenia

Malaxis abieticola
fir-dwelling adder's-mouth

Malaxis bayardii
Bayard's adder's-mouth

Malaxis brachypoda
white adder's-mouth
forma *bifolia*

Malaxis corymbosa
clustered adder's-mouth

Malaxis diphyllos
two-leaved adder's-mouth

Malaxis paludosa
bog adder's-mouth

Malaxis porphyrea
purple adder's-mouth

Malaxis soulei
rat-tailed adder's-mouth

Malaxis spicata
Florida adder's-mouth

Malaxis unifolia
green adder's-mouth
   forma *bifolia*

Malaxis wendtii
Wendt's adder's-mouth

Maxillaria crassifolia
false butterfly orchid

Maxillaria parviflora
densely-flowered maxillaria

Mesadenus lucayanus
copper ladies'-tresses

*Oeceoclades maculata**
spotted African orchis

Oncidium floridanum
Florida oncidium

Pelexia adnata
glandular ladies'-tresses

*Phaius tankervilleae**
nun orchid

Piperia candida
slender white piperia

Piperia colemanii
Coleman's piperia

Piperia cooperi
Cooper's stout-spire orchid

Piperia elegans subsp. *elegans*
elegant piperia
Piperia elegans subsp. *decurtata*
Point Reyes piperia

Piperia elongata
long-spurred piperia

Piperia leptopetala
lace orchid

Piperia michaelii
Michael's piperia

Piperia transversa
flat-spurred piperia

Piperia unalascensis
Alaskan piperia

Piperia yadonii
Yadon's piperia

Platanthera aquilonis
northern green bog orchis
   forma *alba*

Platanthera blephariglottis var.
   blephariglottis
northern white fringed orchis
   forma *holopetala*

Platanthera blephariglottis var.
  conspicua
southern white fringed orchis

Platanthera brevifolia
short-leaved rein orchis

Platanthera chapmanii
Chapman's fringed orchis

Platanthera chorisiana
Chamisso's orchid

Platanthera ciliaris
orange fringed orchis

Platanthera clavellata var. *clavellata*
little club-spur orchis
  forma *slaughteri*
Platanthera clavellata var.
  ophioglossoides
northern club-spur orchis

Platanthera cristata
orange crested orchis
  forma *straminea*

Platanthera dilatata var. *dilatata*
tall white northern bog orchis
Platanthera dilatata var. *albiflora*
bog candles
Platanthera dilatata var. *leucostachys*
Sierra rein orchid

Platanthera flava var. *flava*
southern tubercled orchis
Platanthera flava var. *herbiola*
northern tubercled orchis
  forma *lutea*

Platanthera grandiflora
large purple fringed orchis
  forma *albiflora*
  forma *bicolor*
  forma *carnea*
  forma *mentotonsa*

Platanthera hookeri
Hooker's orchis
  forma *abbreviata*

Platanthera huronensis
green bog orchis

Platanthera hyperborea
northern rein orchis

Platanthera integra
yellow fringeless orchis

Platanthera integrilabia
monkey-face orchis

Platanthera lacera
green fringed orchis, ragged orchis

Platanthera leucophaea
eastern prairie fringed orchis

Platanthera limosa
Thurber's bog orchid

Platanthera macrophylla
Goldie's pad-leaved orchis

Platanthera nivea
snowy orchis

Platanthera obtusata subsp. *obtusata*
blunt-leaved rein orchis
   forma *collectanea*
   forma *foliosa*
Platanthera obtusata subsp. *oligantha*
few-flowered blunt-leaved rein orchis

Platanthera orbiculata
pad-leaved orchis
   forma *lehorsii*
   forma *trifolia*

Platanthera pallida
pale fringed orchis

Platanthera peramoena
purple fringeless orchis

Platanthera praeclara
western prairie fringed orchis

Platanthera psycodes
small purple fringed orchis
   forma *albiflora*
   forma *ecalcarata*
   forma *rosea*
   forma *varians*

Platanthera purpurascens
short-spurred bog orchis

Platanthera sparsiflora
few-flowered rein orchis

Platanthera stricta
slender bog orchis

Platanthera tipuloides var. *behringiana*
Behring orchid

Platanthera zothecina
cloistered bog orchid

Hybrids:
Platanthera ×*andrewsii*
Andrews' hybrid fringed orchis
Platanthera ×*bicolor*
bicolor hybrid fringed orchis
Platanthera ×*canbyi*
Canby's hybrid fringed orchis
Platanthera ×*channellii*
Channell's hybrid fringed orchis
Platanthera ×*correllii*
Correll's hybrid rein orchis
Platanthera ×*estesii*
Estes hybrid rein orchis
Platanthera ×*hollandiae*
Holland River hybrid fringed orchis
Platanthera ×*keenanii*
Keenan's hybrid fringed orchis
Platanthera ×*lassenii*
Lassen hybrid rein orchis
Platanthera ×*reznicekii*
Reznicek's hybrid fringed orchid
Platanthera ×*vossii*
Voss' hybrid rein orchis

Platythelys querceticola
low ground orchid, jug orchid

Platythelys sagreana
Cuban ground orchid

Pleurothallis gelida
frosted pleurothallis

Pogonia ophioglossoides
rose pogonia
   forma *albiflora*
   forma *brachypogon*

Polystachya concreta
pale-flowered polystachya

Ponthieva brittoniae
Mrs. Britton's shadow-witch

Ponthieva racemosa
shadow-witch

Prescottia oligantha
small prescottia

Prosthechea boothiana var.
  erythronioides
Florida dollar orchid

Prosthechea cochleata var. *triandra*
Florida clamshell orchid
  forma *albidoflava*

Prosthechea pygmaea
dwarf butterfly orchid

Pseudorchis straminea
Newfoundland orchis

Pteroglossaspis ecristata
crestless plume orchid
  forma *flava*

Sacoila lanceolata var. *lanceolata*
leafless beaked orchid
  forma *albidaviridis*
  forma *folsomii*
Sacoila lanceolata var. *paludicola*
Fakahatchee beaked orchid
  forma *aurea*

Sacoila squamulosa
hoary leafless beaked orchid

Schiedeella arizonica
red-spot ladies'-tresses

Spathoglottis plicata*
Purple Javanese orchid

Spiranthes amesiana
Ames' ladies'-tresses

Spiranthes brevilabris
**short-lipped ladies'-tresses, Texas
  ladies'-tresses**

Spiranthes casei var. *casei*
Case's ladies'-tresses
Spiranthes casei var. *novaescotiae*
Case's Nova Scotian ladies'-tresses

Spiranthes cernua
nodding ladies'-tresses

Spiranthes delitescens
Canelo Hills ladies'-tresses

Spiranthes diluvialis
Ute ladies'-tresses

Spiranthes eatonii
Eaton's ladies'-tresses

Spiranthes floridana
Florida ladies'-tresses

Spiranthes infernalis
Ash Meadows ladies'-tresses

Spiranthes lacera var. *lacera*
northern slender ladies'-tresses
Spiranthes lacera var. *gracilis*
southern slender ladies'-tresses

Spiranthes laciniata
lace-lipped ladies'-tresses

Spiranthes longilabris
long-lipped ladies'-tresses

Spiranthes lucida
shining ladies'-tresses

Spiranthes magnicamporum
Great Plains ladies'-tresses

Spiranthes ochroleuca
yellow ladies'-tresses

Spiranthes odorata
fragrant ladies'-tresses

Spiranthes ovalis var. *ovalis*
southern oval ladies'-tresses
Spiranthes ovalis var. *erostellata*
northern oval ladies'-tresses

Spiranthes parksii
Navasota ladies'-tresses

Spiranthes porrifolia
western ladies'-tresses

Spiranthes praecox
giant ladies'-tresses
   forma *albolabia*

Spiranthes romanzoffiana
hooded ladies'-tresses

Spiranthes sylvatica
woodland ladies'-tresses

Spiranthes torta
southern ladies'-tresses

Spiranthes tuberosa
little ladies'-tresses

Spiranthes vernalis
grass-leaved ladies'-tresses

Hybrids:
Spiranthes ×borealis
northern hybrid ladies'-tresses
Spiranthes ×folsomii
Folsom's hybrid ladies'-tresses
Spiranthes ×intermedia
intermediate hybrid ladies'-tresses
Spiranthes ×itchetuckneensis
Ichetucknee Springs hybrid ladies'-
   tresses
Spiranthes ×meridionalis
southern hybrid ladies'-tresses
Spiranthes ×simpsonii
Simpson's hybrid ladies'-tresses

Stenorrhynchos michuacanum
Michoacan ladies'-tresses

Tipularia discolor
crane-fly orchis
   forma *viridifolia*

Tolumnia bahamensis
Florida's dancing lady

Trichocentrum carthagenense
spread-eagle orchid

Trichocentrum undulatum
spotted mule-eared orchid
   forma *flavovirens*

Triphora amazonica
wide-leaved noddingcaps

Triphora craigheadii
Craighead's noddingcaps

Triphora gentianoides
least noddingcaps

Triphora rickettii
Rickett's noddingcaps

Triphora trianthophora subsp.
   trianthophora
three birds orchid
   forma *albidoflava*
   forma *caerulea*
   forma *rossii*

Tropidia polystachya
many-flowered tropidia

Vanilla barbellata
worm-vine, leafless vanilla

Vanilla dilloniana
Dillon's vanilla

Vanilla mexicana
scentless vanilla, thin-leaved vanilla

Vanilla phaeantha
oblong-leaved vanilla

*Vanilla planifolia**
commercial vanilla

*Vanilla pompona**
southern vanilla

*Zeuxine strateumatica**
lawn orchid

Paul Martin Brown is a research associate at the University of Florida Herbarium at the Florida Museum of Natural History in Gainesville, Florida. He is the founder of the North American Native Orchid Alliance and editor of the *North American Native Orchid Journal.* Brown and his partner Stan Folsom published *Wild Orchids of the Northeastern United States* in 1997 and *Wild Orchids of Florida* from University Press of Florida in 2001. Questions may be addressed to him at naorchid@aol.com.

Stan Folsom is a retired art teacher and botanical illustrator whose primary medium is watercolor. His work is represented in several permanent collections, including the Federal Reserve Bank of Boston.